EXMOOR VILLA
A to Z

Berta Lawrence

Over 60 places in the National Park described with
their background of wild life, and historical and
literary associations. Illustrated.

The Exmoor Press

First published 1984

ISBN 0 900131 47 0

MICROSTUDIES

Each Microstudy has been written by an expert and is designed to appeal to all those who are interested in Exmoor.

A list of all the titles is available from

The Exmoor Press   Dulverton   Somerset

Front Cover: Horner (courtesy of Exmoor National Park)
Back Cover: Withypool (Michael Deering)

Printed in Great Britain by Williton Printers Ltd., Williton, Somerset.

The Author

Berta Lawrence was born in Buckinghamshire and educated at Aylesbury Grammar School. After taking a London University Bachelor of Arts Degree with First Class Honours, she taught English in a French university and in two French schools. She has spent the greater part of her life in Somerset and most of her books are set against a Somerset background, including two novels and a biography, *Coleridge and Wordsworth in Somerset.*

She has written many children's stories for the BBC, Radio Eireann and the journal, *Child Education,* as well as numerous contributions to a variety of papers and magazines. She is married to John F. Lawrence, co-author with John Hamilton of *Men and Mining in the Quantocks.* She has a son and daughter.

Foreword

This is no ordinary guide book. No map is provided, but the Ordnance Survey National Grid reference is given at the head of each entry. All the villages are located inside — or on the very edge of — the National Park, whose boundary is clearly marked on the O.S. Tourist Map.

Exmoor villages vary as widely as the components of the landscape. and so my purpose is to give you, the reader, the taste of each individual place by describing its appearance, and its background of wild life, history and literary associations. In other words this is a book to savour, to slip into your pocket or bag as you travel round Exmoor, to keep by your bedside. Minehead is excluded as it lies outside the National Park boundary and because a separate Microstudy is devoted to it — *Old Minehead and around*, by Hilary Binding, published by the Exmoor Press. Sources of photographs and quotations in the text are duly acknowledged. Since the book is alphabetical, no Contents pages have been thought necessary. A Select Book List is on pages 117-118.

I wish to express my warmest thanks to David Bromwich of the Local History Library, Taunton, and to Victor Bonham-Carter for help in preparing this book. —B.L.

Landacre Bridge. See p.112.

Mike Naylor

ALLERFORD

When only a handful of Saxon peasants inhabited this pretty place, it must have made an oasis in the huge Exmoor wilderness, with Allerford Water running over the red stones and broadening to make a ford near a grove of alders. No doubt the Saxons threw a wooden bridge across the stream, to be replaced by a stone one over which, for several centuries, the packhorses laboured with their burden of fleeces from Exmoor farms. Almost certainly an inn stood always by the bridge where the Packhorse Inn now stands. This inn, the tiny bridge, the neighbouring red stone cottage with external bread oven and red chimney, make a truly attractive picture. Beyond the bridge a track traverses wooded hill slopes to reach Selworthy, where it emerges near the Tithe Barn. Clement Kille, the Minehead historian, found the remains of an old cobbled track, a real 'church path' running alongside it.

Children coming out of school used to throw stones in the stream, fish in it, sometimes paddle in it, watch wagtail, stone-chat, or an occasional water rat. Cicely Cooper in her book, *Memoirs of Selworthy and West Somerset*, wrote lively chapters about the years she spent there as mistress of the school, which also served Selworthy, and celebrated its 150th birthday on 5 July 1972. Now, alas, it is closed. In 1940 Miss Cooper had 85 pupils and, with a colleague, taught them within earshot of the blacksmith's forge, a place that boys found of perpetual interest, especially when horses came to be shod. The blacksmith's premises are there still, and belong to the Kent family, celebrated since the 18th century as Exmoor smiths. Shoeing is now concentrated at Porlock, Exford and Wootton Courtenay, ornamental ironwork at Porlock, and agricultural engineering at Allerford.

Many other country trades have however disappeared. A directory of 1939 listed a laundry, bootmaker and repairer, market gardener, and shopkeeper, as well as a blacksmith. A directory of 1914 included in addition a fishmonger, dairy produce merchant and gamekeepers and gardeners employed by the Holnicote estate. Early in the present century Mr. Frere, an Allerford artist, sketched the design of angels' heads that a Porlock craftsman, Philip Burgess, executed in embossed leather to cover the base of the reredos in Selworthy church.

Repairs to Miss Cooper's school were carried out by the skilled carpenter from Brandish Street (part of Allerford). It was an indispensible building for the whole parish of Selworthy, which possessed no village hall and used the school for social functions. Almost a century earlier the incumbent of Selworthy visited Allerford school one afternoon with his six-year-old daughter, Marianne, who later in life remembered the visit.

> I do not remember much about the learning. My great delight was in the schoolmistress's chicken. The hens sat in the school cupboards. There were two shelves, one for slates, one for hens. The chickens throve and ran about among the pupils.

Marianne also noted that in a 'nearby parish', the blacksmith drew teeth and, on one occasion, skilfully chopped off a man's poisoned finger.

Pylle's or Piles Mill is a water mill, with an overshot wheel driven by a long leat off the Aller, on the opposite side of the main road. Was this a mill that clacked down to the present century 'ever since 'Domesday Book', like Kipling's? An Allerford mill, rented at 10 pence is indeed mentioned in Domesday. Mrs. Thompson, the parson's wife, made a pretty sketch of the mill in the 1850s, showing its half-door and latticed windows, the tiny footbridge, and a road close to orchards. Marianne, her little girl, was taken there at a time of great frost and saw the water frozen to stillness and the wheel glittering with icicles that Allerford children called 'conker bells'.

BARLYNCH   O.S. 929290

A house of Chanons of thordre of Seynt Augustyne.
I perceive that the Prior of that howse will be and is content to resyne his rome and office of priorschipe . . .
The howse is in dette £40 and yn some rewen and dekey.

So runs the letter written by the King's Commissioner, Dr. Tregonwell, to Thomas Cromwell, after his visit to 'ye religious house at Barlyche in Somerset', about two miles north-east of Dulverton. At that time, just before its dissolution in 1537, this little community of Augustinian canons, founded in the 12th century by William de Saye, lord-of-the-manor of Brompton Regis, comprised only six canons and their prior. Obviously it was very poor, its buildings dilapidated, and it possessed few treasures— beyond 13 tons of lead roofing—for the king's enrichment. What it did possess was a lovely tranquil site in the verdant valley of the river Exe where today the last tumbled stones are hardly visible. Portions of the priory stonework are incorporated in the farmhouse, barn and cottage that occupy the same place by the sparkling river, quite near the road and about a mile above Hele Bridge.

Tennyson drove from Brushford along the valley road to Barlynch and spent an hour or two walking on the banks of the Exe, and looking at the fragmentary walls and arches standing between road and river among the well-watered fields and sylvan slopes.

Several parish churches in the neighbourhood claim to possess some relic from Barlynch. For example, the fine east window in the north aisle of Huish Champflower; likewise one of the bells at Dulverton, which is said to have uttered a mournful cry when loaded on to the wagon for its removal. Since then it has tolled for funerals for many years. It is inscribed: *Protege Virgo Pia quos convoco Sancta Maria.*

Packhorse Bridge, Allerford

V.B.C.

BOSSINGTON
and LYNCH

O.S. 898478

O.S. 902467

At Bossington, willows trail their branches over the central green in company with maples and walnut trees. Some of the walnuts are newly planted, replacing stout old ones reputedly 700 years old, whose gnarled branches over-arched the road and had to be propped up. To the east the steep rounded dome of Bossington Hill and the wooded side of Selworthy Beacon rise up beyond the green. In autumn sunshine the sight of their tawny acres of bracken, their bronze and green foliage, make a traveller linger, just as he will in spring when the trees are bursting into leaf, the air is full of birdsong and the running stream makes music.

The Exmoor naturalist and writer, E. W. Hendy, lived for many years in a cottage in Bossington Lane, and found rich material for his work in the woods, fields, hedgerows and along the coast, as indeed elsewhere on Exmoor. He watched and wrote of the many birds encouraged to come to the bird tables 'beneath our window'— greenfinch, chaffinch, redstart, yellow hammer, once a kestrel even, and in time of snow the black-headed gull. He wrote too of the cuckoo, owl, water ousel, corncrake, and curlew, sometimes corresponding about them with the famous naturalist and author, W. H. Hudson, united with him in a love of birds and Exmoor. Later he recorded the habits of the badger, fox, otter, and red deer, including a fascinating story about an old stag called 'Rufus', who managed to hang himself in a cleft oak in Horner Woods. Combes, orchards, moorland, Dunkery, he wrote them all; and his book *Wild Exmoor through the Year* enables an emigrating West Somerset man to carry a breath of his native air abroad.

At Bossington the lovely Horner stream finds its way to the sea, running and rippling over red brown stones planed smooth by its motion. It flows under a bridge of red sandstone and, when in spate, rushes and roars and whitens with foam. Near its destination, it filters quietly through the broad shelf of grey shingle that curves round Porlock Bay from Gore Point to Hurlstone Point where, less than 6,000 years ago, the rise in the level of the Bristol Channel submerged substantial areas of woodland, mostly oak, yew, pine and alder. That is the meaning of the 'submarine forest' marked on the Ordnance Survey map.

The beach that lies behind the shingle bank was a place favoured by smugglers in Napoleonic times. In his book, *The Somerset Coast,* C. G. Harper tells us that, when a field between Bossington and Porlock was ploughed up, the ploughman discovered a store chamber built about a century earlier. Another version says that the chamber was ten foot square, high as a man, and was found when a hunted hare went below ground.

Swaling at Bossington

David Webb

Lynch lies close to Bossington, on the road to Allerford: the name deriving perhaps from the 'lynches' or terraces created by ploughing sloping hillsides. The grey and russet buildings of this minute hamlet take shelter in a combe where ferns and primroses grow in abundance. Opposite the stream is Lynch chapel built about 1520 to serve the manor of Bossington which, even before the Norman Conquest, belonged to Athelney Abbey in the Somerset marshlands. Like the chapel at Tivington it is a daughter-church of Selworthy. Standing close to the courtyard and outbuildings of the manor house, it served as a barn for three centuries after the Reformation until, again like Tivington, it was rescued from secular use and in 1885 restored for church services by Sir Thomas Acland.

The atmosphere of this little chapel-of-ease is both dignified and intimate. Eleven of the original bosses still adorn the waggon roof, some carved with foliage, some with angels. The lower part of the rough white walls is panelled with oak from old pews brought from Selworthy church in 1930, and oak from the same source made the small west gallery to hold a harmonium. In his book, *Churches and Chapels of Exmoor,* N. V. Allen says that the new pews were made from locally grown oak. Two stone brackets on the east wall, that once supported images of saints, often hold vases of flowers from nearby gardens. The sheltered valley, in which both Lynch and Bossington lie, encourages flowers—fuchsias, hydrangeas, and roses still bloom in early November, some of them outside the house-gate by the chapel.

In her evocative reminiscences, *Memoirs of Selworthy,* Cicely Cooper, formerly the schoolmistress at Allerford, recalls escorting her young pupils to festival services in Lynch chapel. At Easter, Ascensiontide, and Christmas when, as she relates, altar and windows were decked with flowers, foliage and berries, children's voices filled it with the music of Easter hymns or Christmas carols, often accompanied—not only by the harmonium—but by the lowing of oxen or the crowing of cocks on the farm.

When the chapel was deserted after the Dissolution of the monasteries and chantries, at least one carved bench end found its way into the manor house. Various families lived here, and the usual legends sprang up around the more eccentric ones. For example, Mrs. Stoate, a widow, is reputed to have left £10,000 in gold coin, stuffed into drawers and pots.

BRENDON *O.S. 768484*

A large slice of historic Exmoor lies within this parish, including some of the so-called Doone Country—Hoccombe Combe for instance, where R. D. Blackmore saw the remains of the hamlet of Badgworthy, a deserted medieval settlement of about 14 habitations, still traceable today. At the end of the 12th century Badgworthy belonged to the Pomeroy family, who gave to the Brethren of the Hospital of Jerusalem 'the church of Brendon with its appendages and the land of the hermits of Bagawordia'. The last recorded occupation was in 1430, but an occasional poor family may have lived there before the place was finally abandoned. Blackmore drew on these Badgworthy ruins for his description of the Doone Houses in his best-selling novel, *Lorna Doone;* and he deliberately romanticised the topography in creating the Doone Valley, thereby generating endless arguments as to where it exactly was. What is certain however is that Blackmore did not invent the Doone legends, which were well-known in the parish long before he wrote the book.

Fact or fiction the area is populated with Doone sites and stories. For example, it was at the forge (now a guesthouse) close to the old packhorse bridge at Brendon that Jan Ridd saw the smith step outside to dip red hot horse shoes in the Lyn. And on his way to Ley Manor (Lee Abbey), Jan stood on the ivy-covered arch of Hillsford Bridge and watched the confluence of Hoaroak and Farley Waters. Standing there in later years he looked at the road to Farley Water Farm and recalled the adventures of Major Wade, an officer who supported the Duke of Monmouth and became a fugitive after the defeat at Sedgemoor in 1685.

Brendon (meaning 'Bramble Hill') lies north-west of the Doone territory, hugged between steep moors and the East Lyn river that swirls on its way to Lynmouth. The way in from the west, descending through the woods when the oaks burn with autumn colours, is an exhilarating experience. You first pass the church, 700 feet up, 1½ miles distant from the village, and dedicated appropriately to St. Brendan, a Celtic missionary. It was moved from Cheriton in 1738, stone by stone it is said, and the west tower added in 1838. The building is stark and rather isolated, but possesses an ancient font, three bells dated in the 1500s, and a 17th century chalice. It may have served smugglers on occasions in an emergency. Tombstones carry names such as John Crowcombe,

Yeoman, and such simple epitaphs as:

Death with his Dart
In the morning pierced my heart.

Next down the road comes the hamlet of Rockford, with its inn and clutch of attractive cottages, before you reach Brendon itself preceded by a commodious village hall tucked into a corner of the valley, then the straggling village street, the Staghunters' Inn, and the village shop and post office. See picture on the front cover.

High above the village to the south hangs Brendon Common, clad in black, brown and purple, spiked with gorse and thorn, neighbour of The Chains and Exe Plain, gathering grounds of most of Exmoor's rivers. Nine inches of rain fell in 24 hours here on 15-16 August 1952, transforming the rivers into raging torrents and Brendon Common into an inland sea. Many regard this huge area as the true primeval Exmoor, grazed by hardy cattle and sheep, and where Exmoor ponies run in wild liberty.

Brendon Pony Fair goes back probably 200 years. The ponies, all owned and branded by local farmers, are rounded up on the third Saturday in October by riders. Originally they were taken to Cheriton, but now to Leeford Farm in the village. The sale takes place on the following Monday afternoon, any unsold animals used to be driven (now carted in horse boxes) to Bampton for the Fair that takes place there at the end of the month.

BRIDGETOWN—see EXTON

BROMPTON REGIS   O.S. 954314

Haddon Hill on a late summer's day; acres of purple heather and rough grass, thickets of gorse to the north, a quilted landscape where the water of the Wimbleball reservoir lies deep in the lovely valley of the winding Haddeo river under woods of pine, alder and birch. Beyond, a blanket of coloured fields with the towers of Upton old church and St. Mary, Brompton Regis rising above it. The line of pink, grey and white houses with roofs of Brendon slate is the village street of Brompton Regis. In Saxon times when it was called Bruneton, meaning the 'settlement in the Brendons', the place was owned by Githa, Earl Godwin's widow. After her son Harold's death at the Battle of Hastings in 1066, William the Conquerer seized it—hence the name, alternatively Kingsbrompton—and it became part of the manor of William de Saye, founder of Barlynch priory, near Dulverton.

This is a hunting area. Old people say that seventy or more years ago, village children played a game called 'Stag and Hounds' in their dinner hour, which meant truancy in the afternoon when they 'chased' through the heather on Haddon Hill. They also learned the legend that, when the sun rose on Easter morning, they would see a 'lamb in the sun' if they watched from Haddon Hill. One farmer took his two little girls up there early one Easter Day, and indeed they were delighted to find a stray lamb. Other legends of the locality are less gentle. One story says that this village of farmsteads owes the fertility of its fields to the blood and burials of men and horses slaughtered in battle when the inhabitants, armed with reaping hooks and scythes, defended the place against mounted invaders equipped with swords and pikes. No one knows the origin of this tale.

Once a market town—the largest in the area—the village retains few vestiges of its former importance, with a fine church, chapel (once the centre of a Bible Christian circuit), shop, and a pretty white inn, called the 'George', with small window panes and flower baskets hanging on a veranda. Opposite the church there are two cottages with a pump and a recess for a water tap in the garden wall. A plaque dated 1870 is piously inscribed:

Whosoever drinketh of this water shall thirst again, but he that drinketh of Me shall never thirst.

But the blacksmith has gone and a handful of other small industries that were still actively in business in the decade after the last war.

From the church's south porch in the high churchyard you look towards Haddon Hill, feel the air flowing over steeply tilted fields, purple moorland and clumps of trees, and are reminded that this village has access to splendid walks, such as the one leading through Hartford Woods down to Bury. The west tower was built in the 13th century and the fine Perpendicular north aisle added about the year 1520. But the building suffered much at the hands of Victorian restorers who threw out, with the old pews and singers' gallery, a beautiful fan-vaulted rood screen. It was stored in the parson's stable for a time and then sold to a Tiverton dealer in about 1860.

However the building is well cared for and adorned in various ways now: with two large squints that frame vases of flowers and, over one of them, a striking Royal Achievement brilliantly painted with gold lion and white unicorn linked by a gold chain.

The Methodist chapel has the interesting feature of a small balcony looking down upon six rows of seats and a preaching desk in a corner. Also two stained glass windows portraying Balaam with his ass in company with John the Baptist, and separated by a large wooden crucifix, presented by the Joyce family—unusual decorations for a Nonconformist place of worship, but—it is said—the church could not find room for them and the Methodists were more charitable.

Travelling east you soon come to the fine new Bessom Bridge, spanning the tributary that joins the Haddeo above Wimbleball dam and forms the northern arm of the reservoir.

BRUSHFORD   *O.S. 920258*

In 1891 Tennyson and his son, Hallam, made a summer tour through part of Devon and West Somerset. They travelled by train from Exmouth and put up at the Carnarvon Arms Hotel next to Dulverton station (now closed), which is in Brushford parish. Here they spent several happy days taking trips, gentle enough to suit Tennyson's advanced age (he was over 80 and died in the following year), into the lovely countryside around. They were not disappointed, for they had chosen the Dulverton district thanks to acquaintance with Lord Carnarvon of Pixton Park, who had said that 'the streams were the most delicious he knew'.

The tour took them through the entrancing Haddeo valley, along lanes where ragged robin and wild garlic flowered in profusion, and climbed to the crest of Haddon Hill. They followed the windings of the wooded Exe and visited the ruins of Barlynch priory, returning through Dulverton itself and back to Brushford beside the river Barle. On their last night at the hotel their hostess, Mrs. Nelder, hesitantly asked Tennyson to autograph her copy of his *Poems*.

The Carnarvon Arms, built in 1873-4 to serve the railway and as a centre for hunting and fishing, has had many well-known or otherwise remarkable visitors over the past hundred years, including foreigners. Among them was a Frenchman, Monsieur

Ernest Simons, who — before the last war — came over regularly in July to hunt with the 'Devon and Somerset'. In the *Exmoor Review 1968* Mrs. Letty Shoppee recalled that he would bring his huntsman and two of his hunters with him, and in the evenings would often blow hunting calls on the lawn of the hotel. These could be heard at a distance of about two miles as the crow flies, or 'as the cow flies' as he would say. Indeed although he spoke English fluently, he would always translate literally from the French and never lost his Gallic accent. Another friend, Mrs. Monica Eyre, added that on one occasion when he telephoned Exford Stables for a car and a groom, this was interpreted as 'wanting a horse called Dragoon'.

The old and attractive part of Brushford lies round the church of St. Nicholas. The ancient oak in the churchyard is riven, crippled and propped up, but still a fine sight when arrayed in autumn gold. The trunk of another oak, hollowed out, made the roughly fashioned iron-banded chest in the south porch, safeguarded by three locks for the use of the parson and two churchwardens. But there are finer treasures. For example, the beautiful rood screen skilfully carved in the 15th century with vine leaves and other motifs; French and Flemish stained glass in the chancel; a font with a 12th century bowl and some medieval pews at the back of the nave; and— nearer our times—the chapel, designed by Lutyens and built as a memorial to Colonel Aubrey Herbert, scholar and soldier, reputed to have been the model for John Buchan's Sandy Arbuthnot in *Greenmantle*. A modern sculpture of St. Nicholas fills a niche in the north wall of the nave.

Further along the valley on the road to Nightcott and approached by a long drive is Combe, a Tudor house, built on the site of an older house which successive generations altered and enlarged, making a garden out of one of its courtyards. It was occupied by the Sydenham family from 1540 until 1874. In the 17th century Humphrey Sydenham was vicar of Brushford and by his eloquence won the epithet 'silver-tongued'. Under the Commonwealth he was deprived of his living because of his loyalty to Archbishop Laud and Charles I. Tradition holds that Francis Drake played bowls on a green behind the house, and possibly he did, for his young second wife was Elizabeth Sydenham from Monksilver, cousin of the family. Workmen making alterations at Combe found two Armada medals and several Elizabethan coins beneath the porch. A silver and lead mine on the estate was worked until the end of the 18th century, and at one time the owner of Combe possessed a heavy silver candlestick made from its ore and hallmarked 1750.

The year 1685 saw the start of a legend not yet lost. Major George Sydenham, the then owner of Combe, often argued with his friend, Captain Dyke, about the existence of God and the immortality of the soul. They agreed that the first who died would return three nights after the funeral to speak to the other, who must sleep in a little garden house at Combe. The Major died first, and so Captain Dyke asked for the key of the garden and duly slept undisturbed in the garden house. He resumed his merry unbelieving life until, several weeks later, when sleeping in another room, he was disturbed by a ghostly visitant, whom he recognised as his old friend. White and shaking he reported:

I saw him but now. He came and drew my bed curtains aside, saying 'Cap, Cap' — his name for me — and I replied 'What, my Major?'. He said 'I could not come at the time appointed. I come now to tell you there *is* a God, a very just and terrible one. You will find it so if you do not turn over a new leaf'.

Ford and Packhorse Bridge, Bury

J. H. German

BURY

Nowhere looks less suited to a name meaning a 'fortified place' than this tiny hamlet tucked into the lower valley of the River Haddeo, a couple of miles east of Dulverton. The Norman stronghold that designated it has not completely vanished, for the outlines of its motte-and-bailey can still be traced among grass and bluebells under trees on the hill that rises at Bury Castle above the confluence of the Exe and Haddeo. The 18th century historian Collinson, who discovered such hidden places on horseback, states that it was a 'Roman work . . . built on and inhabited by the knightly family of Bésilles'; but no one has been able to confirm this association. It is however the 'Forest Keep' in the novel of that title by Alice King, the blind author who lived at Cutcombe.

Bury is a pretty place to stroll around. There are brown and white houses, some with brick chimneys, and a slate-roofed Methodist Chapel, erected in 1889, bearing the inscription 'Preach the Gospel to every Creature'. The hamlet is bisected by the river ford and a narrow packhorse bridge, described half-a-century ago as 'wide enough to allow a horse and trap to pass over'. On the north side of the water stands a building, first built as the village school in about 1850 by Lady Carnarvon. It was replaced by a larger building in 1890 topped by a bell turret, subsequently converted into an Anglican chapel, and now in use as a private house.

For the walker there is a bridleway of great beauty that runs beside the Haddeo all the way up from Bury to the dam at Wimbleball. Originally constructed as a carriage drive by Lady Harriet Acland at the end of the 18th century, it was vividly described by Col. C. E. Rusbridge in the *Exmoor Review 1974,* before the dam was built. Of Lady Harriet he wrote:

> In her younger days she had accompanied her husband, Major John Dyke Acland, with his regiment to Canada, and when he was wounded and taken prisoner at Saratoga, she went up the Hudson River in an open boat, bearing a letter from General Burgoyne to the American commander, who allowed her to land in his lines to nurse her husband. Through the marriage of her daughter to the 2nd Earl of Carnarvon, all these estates [at Pixton and Wiveliscombe] passed to the Herberts.

Charcoal burners used to ply their trade in the woods on both sides of the river; and slate and stone were quarried as well. Tin mining was even attempted at Clammer. At Hartford, shortly before you reach the dam, the Haddeo is joined by the 'noisy little Pulham river'.

CHALLACOMBE

The village lies in its blue-green combe, the 'cold valley' of the etymologists, folded in rough acres of moorland. Before the era of motorised transport, letters were delivered thrice weekly at the shop for residents to collect when buying groceries and tobacco or bartering eggs and butter. So A. G. Bradley tells us in his *Exmoor Memories* in which, under the fictitious name of Windycombe—'the moorland gales can rock it and rains drench it'—he recalls the village of slate-roofed whitewashed cottages plumed with peat smoke that he saw from a horse-drawn 'fly' one night in the 1860s. The inn, today bearing the exotic name of the Black Venus—so-called, it is said, after a sheep that no one could shear—was the Ring o' Bells then.

Like the modern visitor young Bradley was surprised at the distance that Challacombe people must walk to Holy Trinity Church, 900 feet up on a gale-swept hill at Barton Town, at least a mile from the village and approached by a long beech-hedged lane where little bridges span a stream and noticeboards warn 'Liable to Flooding'. Home Farm is the church's neighbour—stout stone walls, stout pillars to its barns, a stout stone porch at the front door. The church's interior is white, bare, as devoid of monuments as Bradley found it, with a 14th century font, and a wealth of hart's tongue fern growing on the stonework of a window *inside* the tower. Young Bradley was greatly entertained by the performance of Isaac, the grotesque and diminutive parish clerk, who tootled on a flute and, with his three sons, provided a choir of 'husky peasant voices' to sing Tate and Brady's metrical psalms. Isaac reposes in the churchyard among other 'forefathers of the hamlet': names such as Pugsley, Webber, Ridd, Leworthy, and Huxtable are on the headstones; some of the girls were called Charity, Dorcas or Agnes. One Huxtable—and his sons after—worked the mill and was a carpenter as well. A daybook, discovered by the antiquarian, Charles Whybrow, recorded 'Mad a Cofin for Susanna Jones' for one day in July 1824. Edward Webber, famous local wrestler, was buried here in 1847, aged 102.

One Sunday morning James Hannington, then curate at Martinhoe, rode his pony for several hours up and down the moorland in dense mist and rain as he tried to find Challacombe church where he was due to take the service. He eventually found the congregation waiting with Christian patience. 'Be short, as us all wants to get back to dinner', the clerk admonished him loudly.

In Bradley's day hardly any of the moorland had been reclaimed. He loved it for its wealth of wild life—fox, badger, buzzard, adder, raven, the blackcock he was taught to shoot, and the brawling brown streams that provided him with splendid fishing. The place is surrounded with evidence of bygone man: Chapman Barrows and the Longstone to the north, Shoulsbury Castle to the south, and many other tumuli, stones and circles about which folk lore wove stories of 'conjurors', and buried treasure, of doom, curses and death, and of the tramplings of ghostly horsemen and warriors. A stone cannon ball unearthed at Home Farm generated a comparatively modern legend about Prince Charles (later Charles II) who, after a skirmish with Roundhead Troops, took refuge in a rude shelter built for him at Mole's Chamber.

There is also a tradition that the two last members of the Doone family, a grandfather and his little grand-daughter, died one Christmas Eve after singing carols 'for pennies' in Challacombe. Their bodies were found in the snow on the road to Simonsbath.

Challacombe at New Year

Colin Thornton

19

CLOUTSHAM and HORNER

O.S. 892431
O.S. 899454

Cloutsham is neither a village nor a hamlet but a farm well known to everyone who has ever hunted the red deer on Exmoor. It is reached by a zig-zag road up from Webber's Post or over the top from Stoke Pero Common. The opening meet of the Devon and Somerset Staghounds in late summer, a special hunting occasion, makes a spectacle of movement and colour against the background of heather-purpled slopes, and the dense woods at Horner and other parts of the Holnicote estate planted by the Acland family in the 19th century. Over a mile away Dunkery Beacon towers to 1704 feet. Another striking feature is Coutsham Ball, vividly described by Richard Jefferies who was brought to Cloutsham by Exmoor friends when he came collecting material for his book, *Red Deer,* in 1883. He described it as

... a round green hill standing by itself in the midst of the dark heather-covered moors ... In shape it resembles a skull cap of green velvet imitated in sward, or it might be a great tennis-ball cut in two. This is Cloutsham Ball ... like a green ball among the surrounding heather, contrasting in its colour and in its form with the moors. So round and smooth ... had it been carved with the chisel it could hardly have been more regular.

With keen eyes this great naturalist-writer painted the scene in words of intimate precision — and then he saw the stag.

Suddenly, as I looked once more, I caught sight of a red mark in the midst of an acre of brake surrounded by oak. I was sure it was a stag instantly by the bright colour, by the position ... He was standing in the fern beside a bush, with his head down as if feeding. The great oak woods were about him, above and below, and the sunlight fell on the golden red of his coat. A whistle — the sound was a moment or two reaching him — made him lift his head, and the upright carriage of the neck proved once again that it was a stag and not a hind. His antlers had not yet risen as high as his ears. Another whistle — he lifted his head yet higher but did not move, for he knew he was safe. The whistle sounded to him faint across the hollow space, and his keen eyes and still keener nostrils assured him that there was no danger.

And of the farm itself:

The old thatched house ... has a hearth as wide as that of a hunting lodge should be, and an arched inner doorway of oak. A rude massiveness characterises the place.

When Jefferies was writing, the roof was thatched, a covering much favoured by Sir Thomas Acland, despite the dangers. The family house at Holnicote had been burned down in 1851 and Cloutsham caught fire in 1915.

A hunting parson, the Rev. H. J. Marshall, who was appointed curate of Porlock in 1895, devoted a whole chapter to Cloutsham in his book, *Exmoor, Sporting and Otherwise,* and remarked *inter alia* on the kitchen, presided over by Susan, wife of the tenant and harbourer, John Lang.

Occupying one side of the kitchen is the open hearth on which a peat fire burns. Summer and winter it never goes out. It serves all purposes: baking bread, cooking meals, scalding the great pans of cream, heating cauldrons of water, curing hams, hung in rows from the oaken beams.

On one occasion, Susan's famous teas of Devonshire cream proved too much for the Field. It happened this way. We had a long day's wait. About three o'clock hunting folk dropped into the farm kitchen for tea until every available place was full. The hopes of a run dropped to zero. All were intent on enjoying the good things spread before us, followed by a quiet jog homeward in the cool of the evening. When all had fed, too well if not too wisely, a shout was heard; 'The stag has gone away'! Among a chorus of groans the company rose and made for their mounts. Lashings of clotted cream and whortleberry jam and cake are an ill fare for a fast burst across Exmoor.

Books and essays about Exmoor hunting are plentiful, and so there is room for only one more reference here, nearer to today. In his volume of stories, *The Old Stag*, Henry Williamson includes a splendid account of an unconquerable stag who ran all day from Cloutsham Wood ('Stumberleap Wood') to Heddons Mouth, and then took to the sea. Williamson paints an arresting picture of wild Exmoor country taking in Cloutsham, the Ball, and Lucott Ridge. The farmhouse of the 1930s was presented as a long stone building roofed with yellow-lichened slates and possessing 'great square chimney tuns', growing ferns in their cracks.

E. W. Hendy, the naturalist, once climbed Dunkery to see the sun rise on 29 May, Oak Apple Day, and wrote an account of his excursion in *Wild Exmoor through the Year*.

We started at a quarter to three; it was almost but not quite dark, for in these short midsummer nights there is always a hushed glimmer of twilight . . . At three-thirty, when we had climbed about nine hundred feet, we heard our first nightjar: its churring was borne to us on a chill east wind over a coombe whose depths were still lost in shadow: another answered in the distance; and from the furze bushes came the chatter of stonechats, a disjointed, jerky warble, as though they were only half awake . . . Just before we reached the top, the sun rose, and peered, red-eyed and sleepy, through clouds stretched like a skein athwart Selworthy Beacon and North Hill. It was a sulky sun-rise.

He and his companion descended the combe alongside Horner Water, verdant with spring foliage, and heard the song of innumerable birds: warbler, blackcap, chaffinch, goldfinch, and the laughing cry of the green woodpecker. Lower down the valley he passed Horner Mill. Today this russet-brown building, half-covered by moss and ivy is silent, its leat is dry. Jefferies wrote:

Where the woods cease and the coombe opens stands Horner Mill, which has a large iron overshot wheel exposed at the side of the building. Deer running down the stream usually break from it as they come to the hatch just above the mill-wheel, and go round the mill, which blocks their course along the brook. Once a hind closely followed was so beset by the hounds that, unable to quit the brook, she leaped from the sluice on to the top of the revolving wheel. The immense iron wheel carried her over and threw her to the ground, disabling her. She was immediately killed to prevent suffering.

The size of this and other water wheels is always impressive. In a chapter contributed to *The Waters of Exmoor* by N. V. Allen, D. W. Warren, an expert in water power, remarked that out of 59 farms on Exmoor found to have wheels, all, with one exception of a breast wheel, were overshot and varied in diameter from 12 to 18 feet and from 2 to 3 feet in width. The 18-foot wheel at Horner was 6 feet wide.

Artists have revelled in the scene. Lionel Edwards learned about it in every season and mood, and executed inimitable paintings of the deer in their green fastnesses inside Horner woods. At the end of a November day spent painting this lovely valley under slopes hung with autumn-coloured woods, A. J. Munnings wrote:

I sat on a stone arch over Horner Water and ate my lunch to the tune of the stream — copper and gold all around.

Beside the harbour at Combe Martin

Rev. W. A. Bevis

COMBE MARTIN
O.S. 585465

Strictly speaking Combe Martin lies just outside the National Park boundary that strikes the sea a short way to the north-east at Lester Point, between Sandy Bay and Wild Pear Beach. The scenery is impressive with Little Hangman (716 feet) and Great Hangman (1,043 feet) thrusting up above the sea, east of Combe Martin Bay. Indeed high hills run inland on both sides of the valley into which the village is wedged. In his book, *The North Devon Coast,* S. H. Burton refers to the 'fascinating network of typical Devon lanes leading out of the village to the heights of the two Hangmen', and to the ferns, mosses and lichens growing abundantly under the high banks and in the ravines of the hills.

As to the village itself, described by Charles Kingsley as 'the mile-long manstye', it is now nearer two miles long than one. Be that as it may, Combe Martin is of ancient origin, being mentioned in Domesday, while the manor was named after one Robert FitzMartin, whose descendants held it until the 14th century. With a harbour so small that it barely justifies the name, it used nevertheless to be busy with craft carrying umber and bark to the Bristol tanneries and, until relatively recently, with the export of strawberries—raised locally on the fertile slopes—to Swansea, borne by a steamer known as the *Snowflake,* described by Vernon C. Boyle in *Devon Harbours* as a 'tubby, grubby, quaint and comic little ship'. Hemp was also a popular crop in the past and spun into shoemakers' thread.

But Combe Martin's main wealth was dug out of the lead and silver mines, explored and exploited at least since the reign of Edward I (1272-1307). In his *A View of Devonshire,* Thomas Westcote recorded that silver cups, fashioned from Combe Martin silver and inscribed with verses, were presented to Queen Elizabeth I and the Lord Mayor of London. Old shafts and adits and ruins of mine buildings still abound and, as recently as September 1983, a warning was given about the possible collapse of some cottages under renovation in the village, and believed to be standing directly over an old 700-foot deep shaft, last used in 1847.

Far the finest building is the parish church of St. Peter Ad Vincula, built of sandstone, with a 99-foot high battlemented tower. It displays Gothic at its best and has many striking features: for instance, a beautiful carved screen dividing nave and chancel, and another section secluding the Lady Chapel in the north aisle. There are other treasures—a marble 17th century effigy of Judith Hancock (Ivatt); a Bishop's chair of great age; and an octagonal font. Among former rectors was John Blackmore, grandfather of R. D. Blackmore, creator of *Lorna Doone*.

The oddest building in the village is The Pack of Cards Inn, formerly the King's Arms, said to have acquired its present name as the result of a fortune won at cards by one of the Ley family. Its extravagant architecture certainly resembles the kind of 'card house' that children construct—or used to.

In his book *Exmoor Memories* A. G. Bradley recalled the Combe Martin of his boyhood in the 1860s—'an earthly paradise' that no outsider visited. When the horses had been put up 'at a large and shabby inn resembling a house of cards', he and the Challacombe Rectory boys joined the family from Combe Martin Rectory for a lunch 'spread on the rocks when the ladies had unpacked cook's hamper'. Afterwards the boys scrambled round coves, 'clinging to the foot of cliffs against which the tide would be surging . . . hanging on to cracks in the rocks with toes and fingers. If our dear mamas could have seen!'

Other writers connected with Combe Martin include Charles Kingsley and R. D. Blackmore already mentioned, but there is yet another—Marie Corelli—whose books are rarely read today, although 80 years ago her hysterical, highly flavoured, romances were gobbled up by readers at every level of society. Her *The Mighty Atom* (1896) had Combe Martin as its scenario and at least one character based on fact—that of Reuben Dale, modelled on James Norman, the sexton of St. Peter's. One can only hope that Mr. Norman benefited from some of the many fans who came to gape at the venue of the novel, that ran into 48 editions.

COUNTISBURY O.S. 747488

Robert Southey riding on horseback from Porlock to Lynton in 1799 was justifiably angry at the stupidity of his guide for not taking him along the coastal route so that he missed 'many noble scenes' embracing cliffs falling a thousand feet to the sea, jagged rocks, hanging woods, deep combes, hill slopes coloured by gorse and heather—that is, some of the best coastal scenery in England, and meat and drink to Romantic poets and men of letters. Furthermore,

'I lost the Danish encampment where Hubba besieged Oddune. We pass the spot where Kenwith Castle stood.'

Southey was referring to Countisbury Castle, the massive Iron Age fortress at Wind Hill, a promontory that falls precipitously away to the south and west, and on the eastern side is protected by a deep ditch and a 30-foot rampart of earth. When crowned with a palisade, it must have been impregnable. A thousand years after it was constructed, by which time it must have been substantially reduced by wind and weather, it was used again in battle. Historians believe it may be the fortress Arx Cynuit, recorded in the *Anglo-Saxon Chronicle* as the place where, in AD 878, King Alfred's besieged forces under Ealdorman Odda rushed downhill, fighting 'like boars' to hurl back 800 invading Danes, killed their leader Hubba, and captured their Raven banner.

The little church of St. John the Evangelist stands nearly 1,000 feet high, on the edge of Foreland Point, Grey and windswept among the yews, it has needed constant repair in order to survive. Faithful parishioners have done all this and more. The nave was rebuilt in 1796, the tower in 1835, the chancel and a new north aisle added in 1846, thanks to the munificence of the Rev. W. S. Halliday of Glenthorne. An interesting account of the place can be found in the first volume of *Reminiscences and Reflections of an Old West Country Clergyman* by the Rev. W. H. Thornton. Thornton served as curate there 1854-6 on a stipend of £20 p.a., eked out with a private income of £200 or so. He combined business with pleasure and revelled in the outdoor life.

Nothing came amiss, and I would walk, ride, shoot, fish, and drive with anybody. I was great, moreover, on the cliffs, and was never tired of risking my life, often alone, hanging and clinging in mid-air on the Foreland, seeking for eggs.

I was keen in my parish work, also . . . Countesbury was handed over to me absolutely, week-day and Sunday alike, with its school and two hundred and fifty inhabitants.

At once I laid my hands upon the school. It was two miles away, on the summit of Countesbury Cliff. It was kept by Mrs. Elworthy, the widow of a butcher of Lynmouth, and she knew positively nothing. It was never inspected, no one cared for it, and few children attended it.

In a very short time he bought books, engaged help, taught every morning and several afternoons, and increased the attendance to 40 pupils. They must have been sad to see him go to become the first incumbent of the newly formed Exmoor parish, based on Simonsbath.

Today the church, a few cottages, and the Blue Ball compose the hamlet of Countisbury. The 16th century inn preserves its black beams, its thick walls and recessed windows, its wide open hearth. Toby jugs that include Winston Churchill and Henry VIII hang in profusion from the beams. It is a cheerful place for walkers, motorists and others on their way to the National Park Information Centre at County Gate; or perhaps to attend Evening Prayer on a second Sunday or a 'Candlelit Epilogue' in the summer. The church contains memorials to the Snow and Fry families, reminding us that the wonderful sweep of landscape includes the Doone Country. See picture on the back cover.

CULBONE   O.S. 843483

Here stands one of the smallest parish churches in England, closeted with two cottages on a green plateau, backed by wooded hills that cut off the sun. A stream runs past, breaking into cascades. There is always the sound of water and the rustle of leaves. This tiny church captivates its many visitors by its littleness and loneliness. It is only 35 feet long, with a waggon roof, stout Norman walls, a shingled spire, two bells (one cast in the 14th century), and a small oak screen six centuries old. Cared for, adorned with flowers, it has a devoted attendance. Once called Kitnor, a name deriving from the Saxon *cyta* and *ore*, interpreted as either a 'cave by the sea' or a 'hill-slope frequented by kites', it has long borne the name of the Celtic missionary from Wales to whom it is dedicated. Culbone is a corruption of ' Kil Beun', or 'the church of St. Bruno'.

An almost secret place, set between the sea and the hilltops rising to 1300 feet, it is difficult of access even now. Motorists must take the toll road that, from Ashley Combe gateway, curves and climbs on a lovely course through the woodlands, then from Silcombe they must walk nearly a mile. Walkers can start from Porlock Weir and follow the steep and narrow track—an old packhorse path—that zig-zags its way high above the sea, in and out of dense woods of oak, beech. chestnut, fir and mountain ash. Ever since the 18th century travellers have described the path with exaggerated adjectives — 'precipitous', 'declivitous', 'hazardous'.

This is the path that Coleridge followed with the Wordsworths — all in their twenties — on their way to Lynton one sunless November day in 1797. 'Our road lay through woods rising almost perpendicularly from the sea,' wrote Dorothy Wordsworth. Coleridge had climbed this way in solitude when the woods blazed with autumn colour, making for Ash Farm. Up this path he and Wordsworth brought their friend Cottle in glorious May weather in 1798, discussing their recently written poems that Cottle was about to publish as the *Lyrical Ballads*. That same month Coleridge tramped the path en route to Lynton talking endlessly to 19-year-old William Hazlitt — a Shropshire lad — and the tongue-tied admiring John Chester from Nether Stowey. In the thick woods they trod on yellow reindeer moss, possibly sighting deer or feral goats — even a wild cat in those days — and noticing a foxhole or badger's sett.

In 1799 the Rev. Richard Warner visited Culbone and recorded his impressions in *A Walk through Some of the Western Counties of England*. At that time the parish had about a dozen houses and some steep cultivated fields, and the churchyard was often the scene of a vigorous Revel. Warner was buttonholed by a garrulous old blacksmith who told him of an experience of his 'about forty-five years agone, Sir'. The Revel was in progress. The blacksmith, full of liquor, had lost all his money plus sixteen shillings out of a guinea borrowed from a friend. His wife had just been brought to bed and he cursed himself for a fool and a scoundrel. Thereupon he bathed his head in the stream and, with the remaining five shillings and a clear head, he bowled straight as a die, recovered all he had lost and repaid the debt. He had never gambled since. Warner was suitably impressed.

Culbone Church

Susan Wintsch

27

In 1872 the Rev. Frederick Hastings, a Congregational minister from Weston-super-Mare, keen on cycling (though hardly the best way to reach Culbone) left a nice story about the church. Apparently the bells were formerly pulled by hay bands instead of ropes, and one day an ox, finding its way within the tower, began eating the rope, ringing the bell at a most unaccustomed hour. In recent times the Scottish artist, Waistel Cooper, and his wife, Joan, lived in one of the two cottages at Culbone — really a lodge of several storeys. They created beautiful pottery and attracted a regular clientele of visitors and buyers. A striking feature of their ware was the silken-smooth glaze obtained by the use of wood ash from burning old thatch, leaves and garden clippings. The Coopers' neighbours were Tom and Lizzie Cook, famous for their homely conversation and magnificent cream teas, for which they insisted on charging unbelievably low prices, long after inflation and decimalisation had galloped away with the profit. Their parlour was decorated with hundreds of cards from well-wishers all over the world.

There are still tracks of the charcoal burners who lived and worked in the woods between Culbone and Glenthorne. It is believed that in the Middle Ages they were a colony of lepers, forbidden to cross to the Porlock side of Culbone water, and for whom a 'leper's window' in the church allowed worship without contaminating the congregation. Sawyers and tanners were also at work in the woods; but all these have long disappeared, leaving Culbone to its solitude and its secrets.

CUTCOMBE and WHEDDON CROSS   O.S. 932394
O.S. 925388

Eighteenth century historians noticed the poorness of the soil and the slavish attitude of Cutcombe's 450 inhabitants. For the latter they blamed the repressive authority of the chief landowner, Sir Philip Hales, of Brymore, Cannington. This man was the 'titled Dogberry', hated by the young Coleridge for conniving at an investigation of the Wordsworths (suspected for their sympathies with the ideals of the French Revolution), who perhaps remembered Hales when they made their long walk through Cutcombe to Dulverton in 1797. They certainly noticed the beauty of the village's surroundings as even its critics did: 'a fruitful vale, bounded by lofty eminence, deep valleys, woodlands, meadows', and in the hamlet of Codsend the infant River Quarme, babbling, silvery, rich in trout, haunted by heron and kingfisher. For centuries Cutcombe was a remote place, yet not remote enough for the Black Death to miss it in 1348, when several people died of it, including the 'poor clerk' (parish clerk). In 1714 the parish benefited from the generosity of a more kindly landowner, Richard Elsworth of Timberscombe who, before dying in his early twenties, endowed Cutcombe with £10 p.a. to build a school for the teaching of reading, writing, and the catechism.

The road climbing Cutcombe Hill from Timberscombe lies under banks where rocks jut out among greenery. Here a little source trickles down a rock face. A Victorian baby, Alice, was baptised with its water, and—when adult—she had a drinking trough installed for horses toiling uphill. The place is called 'Alice's Fountain'. Alice King, whose father was vicar here for 55 years, became blind at the age of seven, yet grew up a quite remarkable woman versed in languages, well-read thanks to a devoted sister, able to knit fine silk in complicated patterns, play the guitar, and type. She rode an Exmoor pony called 'Colly', the West Somerset name for a blackbird. She made long excursions on foot with her sister, enjoying rain, mist and wind as well as sunshine, absorbing the Exmoor scene and details of people's lives through touch and hearing. In her teens she published the first of a number of romantic novels, *Forest Keep*. These, with her essays on historical figures, gave her contact with Mrs. Henry Wood and other popular writers. She left an invaluable record of local life: the shearing feast, whortleberry-picking for the dyers, the Mumming play on Old Christmas Eve (5 January), the binding of the last sheaf at harvest, consultations with the Wise Woman who handled adders, brewed herbal remedies, and saved cattle from evil 'overlooking'. At festivities villagers danced the Handkerchief Dance, the Fox Hunt, the Lady's Breast Knot. They went to the cattle shed on Old Twelfth Night to hear the 'master-bullock' solemnly low three times before sinking to his knees.

The rather grim-looking church, dedicated to St. John, perching above magnificent views to the east, was central to Alice King's life, so that she recorded practices connected with it that have long vanished, with their grace and poetry, in our sophisticated century.

29

Village musicians played clarinets and flutes in the west gallery, and led processions of the Friendly Society. The sexton, wearing a red kerchief on his head, put up the 'Christmassing' (berries and evergreens). At Midsummer girls seeking a bridegroom scattered hempseed in the churchyard. At weddings bachelors strung a rope of flowers across the church gateway; and there were many more such customs sadly gone.

A later incumbent of Cutcombe, the Rev. Arthur Courtenay Jenoure, gained national publicity when, from the pulpit he thundered out his conviction that Mollie Phillips, a local girl who had met her death in mysterious circumstances, had been murdered. Mollie had left her home at Exford on Sunday afternoon 8 September 1929 and then disappeared. Fifteen months later her body was discovered in a bog on Codsend Moor. The cause of her death was never established. The story is told in detail by Jack Hurley in *Murder and Mystery on Exmoor*.

The neighbouring hamlet of Wheddon Cross is cut in half by what Laurence Meynell referred to as 'surely well up in the list for the worst cross-roads in England'. In fact Wheddon Cross stands at the highest point on the road from Dulverton to Dunster and overlooking two river valleys down which the Avill flows north into the sea, and the Quarme south to join the Exe at Coppleham Cross. The inn beckons the Exmoor traveller with the beguiling sign 'Rest and be Thankful'. There is a fine playing field, opposite which stands the Methodist Chapel that replaced an earlier building in 1893. Methodism has had a vigorous history at both Cutcombe and Wheddon Cross. In the last century William Thorne was active for 50 years as a travelling grocer and local preacher, while John Kent was known as the 'apostle of the hill country'. Two other men became missionaries. The Rev. Henry Gulliford did long service in India, and the Rev. H. Baker went to South Africa. The former's father was a clockmaker, and made the sundial which can still be seen on his house in Wheddon Cross.

Several roads meet on the high ridge here. For many years they have brought farmers, shepherds and flocks from all over Exmoor to Cutcombe Sheep Fair in early autumn when thousands of beasts are auctioned—Exmoor Horn, Devon Closewool, hardy Scotch Blackface and Cheviots—a great Exmoor gathering worthy of Thomas Hardy.

DULVERTON

Popular as it is with visitors, Dulverton retains an unaffected country character without self-conscious preservation. In street and store, past and present happily mingle. Restaurants with names like Copper Kettle flourish in company with old inns, the Rock, the Bridge, the Lion with gilded lions couched on its porch, the Lamb with a lamb standing on its Ionic portico. Blackmore's Jan Ridd and John Fry ate prime mutton at an un-named Dulverton inn:

And now John Fry strode into the hostel, with the air and grace of a short legged man, and shouted as loud as if he was calling sheep upon Exmoor —
'Hot mootton pasty for twoo trarv'lers, at number vaive, in vaive minnits! Dish un up in the tin with the grahvy, zame as I hardered last Tuesday.'

Gift shops, grocers, a butcher, antiques, a chemist, a bookshop, fruit and vegetables, a newsagent, etc., all co-exist happily with other shops supplying riders and fishermen — of the kind that Richard Jefferies noticed — and with individual craftsmen who, until recently, included a bespoke bootmaker, saddler, tailor, and a German horologist whose wife painted clock faces.

Writing in *Exmoor Review 1966,* J. M. Slader remarked that Dulverton is surrounded by history — as indeed it is. Iron Age forts at Oldberry Castle (at the southern end of Burridge Wood), Mounsey Castle and Brewer's Castle (some 3 miles up the River Barle). The Norman fortification at Bury Castle, overlooking the junction of the Exe and Haddeo; and Barlynch Priory, founded in the 12th century and dissolved at the order of Henry VIII. Although Page surmised that its name was Celtic, meaning 'the ford town at the bend of the river', he found 'nothing of great interest in Dulverton', and added '. . . after diligent search, I cannot ascertain that it has been the scene of any stirring event.' But Page was looking in the wrong direction, for history is not all composed of 'stirring events', certainly not social history, which is concerned with the way people live and work together, and with the customs and institutions they create.

Dulverton for example, was the home of several great families who lived nearby — the Aclands and then the Carnarvons and the Herberts at Pixton, the Sydenhams at Combe, the Stucley Lucas at Baronsdown, the Mildways at Hollam; and as a centre for hunting and fishing, it attracted — particularly in the last century — a host of enthusiasts some well-known, some not, who came for the sport.

One of the best remembered was a resident, Charles Palk Collyns (1793-1864), author of the classic, *The Chase of the Wild Red Deer*. Educated at Blundells School, Tiverton, he qualified as a 'surgeon apothecary' (general practitioner) and set up his plate in Dulverton in 1814.

As for staghunting, had it not been for Collyns' activities in keeping the hounds in being, the red deer would have been poached out of existence long before 1855, when Mordaunt Fenwick Bisset took over and put the sport on a sound basis. Collyns is remembered by a tablet in the parish church, to which his son gave the organ.

Several other writers, most of them better known, knew Dulverton. Richard Jefferies, for instance. Collecting material in 1883 for his *Red Deer,* while mortally ill, he was yet charmed by the town. He walked alongside the lively Barle below massed woods 'filled with the June colour of oaks.' Oak and ash, ferns, plants, rocks, trout, ousel, pheasant, all delighted him, but above all he loved the vigorous river after watching it

running over red rocks . . . The brown Barle splashes in the sunshine like boys bathing — like them he is sunburnt and brown. He laughs and talks, and sings louder than the wind in his woods.

In their twenties, Wordsworth and his sister, Dorothy, passed through Dulverton, with Coleridge on a long walk in grey November weather. W. H. Hudson happily followed the course of the Exe which, he said 'sings all the way to Dulverton'. Froude, the historian, came on a visit to Pixton Park, his host taking him on drives through the countryside. Whyte-Melville, author of *Katerfelto,* hunted with a Dulverton friend and sometimes rode back with him to gather information on customs and traditions. He put Dulverton 'Revel' into his book about the wonderful grey stallion, named after a mysterious doctor Constantine Katerfelto, which roamed the moors in liberty and sired wonderful progeny. Tennyson and his son, Hallam, visited Dulverton in 1891, the year before he died. Of course, R. D. Blackmore knew the town well.

The church of All Saints, finely situated above the centre of the' town, was drastically restored in 1855, when it lost some interesting features, gallery, box pews, and a 15th century screen. One of the eight bells is supposed to have come from Barlynch. Some of the stained glass was given by Sir George Williams, founder of the Y.M.C.A., who was brought up at Ashway Farm. In the graveyard, the singer Bertram Binyon, brother of the poet Laurence, is buried among clipped yews and hoary stones, and in a carpet of celandines and daffodils reborn every spring. A sycamore called the Belfry Tree — because it stood close to the tower — spread shade for 250 years, now alas a gnarled stump. A chapel-of-ease, built by John Arthur Locke of Northmoor, once stood beside Marsh Bridge, a mile or so north of the town, but it was mysteriously burnt down in c. 1900. The Congregational Chapel, a handsome building with its manse, dated 1831, stands in Milhams Lane. All over the town there are still hidden courts, narrow streets, cobbled alleys and terraces, with ancient names such as Lady street, Addlemead, Hangman's Alley. Although under pressure for widening to accommodate the heavy summer traffic, these are the features that help to give it character.

In its day the Leat, that starts and ends with the River Barle, drove the wheels of at least four mills; a paper mill in Lady Street; the Town Mills (so-called because of its twin breast wheels) which operated as a grist mill; the present and active laundry (formerly a crepe mill, and before that a woollen mill); and, below that, another mill, now called Mill House. At the bottom of the town, at the far end of a pleasant stretch of lawn, stands Exmoor House, now the headquarters of the Exmoor National Park Authority. Once the workhouse, its long and sombre story is told by Jack Hurley in his book, *Rattle His Bones*.

Dulverton Town Hall

Geoffrey N. Wright

33

DUNKERY O.S. 892415

From the summit of Dunkery—at 1,704 feet, the highest point on Exmoor—the climber's gaze takes in the whole range of country rolling towards Dartmoor, or northwards over the Bristol Channel to Wales. It is a poetic place, whether capped with thunder cloud, marbled by snow, shrouded in rain, or soaring bare into blue air when its stony cairns stand out clear-cut. On its head lie the rough unhewn stones of ancient fire-hearths where beacons flared the alarm in time of national danger (as in 1588), were kindled for national rejoicing, and—according to Blackmore—lit the way home for the Doones after a foray. Beacons were lit also on the Rowbarrows on the western ridge, as well as on Joaney Howe and Robin Howe to the north-east. Like Bronze Age men who built them, modern climbers like to add a stone to the cairn-pile at the top.

Many streams rise on Dunkery. On wettest ground the rushes grow with rare mosses and the round-leaved sundew; cotton grass tufts it with white. In drier spots the whortleberry flourishes, harvested locally for centuries. The cranberry has grown rare. Heather covers many acres, often concealing coiled adders. Here roam the ponies, horned sheep, and deer; the stag 'bells' under the autumn moon; fox and badger emerge at night. The buzzard planes overhead in the wind and sun. Naturalists love Dunkery, as do walkers, riders, hunting people, artists and writers.

For example, Dunkery looms over the landscape in Henry Williamson's fine story of Stumberleap, the old stag, and in Tunnicliffe's splendid illustrations. The doomed lover in Thomas Hardy's poem, *The Sacrilege,* roamed with his love 'for one mad moon' where 'Dunkery frowns on Exon Moor'. Collinson wrote of Dunkery 'It rises in naked sublimity'; Savage 'It affords a noble prospect'. Page recorded that, in *Home Chimes* of 5 March 1885, Alice King, the blind novelist of Cutcombe, told a pathetic tale about a ruined cottage on the side of Dunkery.

It was in persecuting days the refuge of two Huguenot ladies, whose extreme poverty caused many remarks in the countryside, nothing but a small quantity of bread being seen to enter their cottage, which was ever jealously guarded from intrusion. After a time they disappeared, and the cottage was visited. Dead and fast locked in each other's arms were the poor refugees. The house was of course searched for comestibles, but nothing was found beyond some pots containing *slugs*, on which, say the people, the exiles had subsisted.

DUNSTER

How to write briefly of Dunster—the crown of Exmoor villages, rich in history and beauty, a miniature town rather than a village? The Castle, founded by William de Mohun and lived in by the Luttrell family for 600 years, is the hill that gave Dunster its Domesday name of Torre. It dominates the little town that Hazlitt, tramping a hilltop with Coleridge in June 1798, described as 'looking clear, as pure, as embrowned as any landscape by Poussin'.

Another tower rises from the woods on a neighbouring hill called Conygar, the old coney-warren of the Castle. This folly was designed in 1776 for a Luttrell by Richard Phelps, the Porlock-born artist; the expenses included £54 for the workmen's cider. Phelps obtained other Dunster commissions. He restored an altar-piece portraying the Crucifixion in the church, and painted several Luttrell portraits including two of Margaret Fownes Luttrell which hang in the Castle and are eclipsed by the fine portrait Reynolds made of her. The once-fashionable portrait-painter Thomas Hudson, born in Dunster, taught the young Reynolds for a short time, and painted the portrait of Anne Luttrell wearing a feathered hat, seen in the drawing-room of the castle.

What a pageant of humanity has unrolled inside the Castle walls and in the narrow streets lined by a collection of buildings (medieval, Tudor, Georgian) above which rises the tower of the lovely church built by John Marys, the Stogursey master-builder. Today it showers from its chimes airs both sacred and secular, ranging from *O Rest in the Lord* to *Drink to Me Only* and the Dunster carol at Christmas. Walls and streets have seen soldiers from Agincourt in whose days the Mohuns built the iron-plated castle gateway, where 19th century workmen found the walled-in skeleton of a manacled giant: medieval masons hauling tackle for building church and priory: Benedictine monks: woodcarvers who made the richly decorated rood screen to divide the nave of the church from the choir, the masterpiece in a group of screens: seamen who sailed a ship called *Leonard of Dunster* and used the vanished port called Dunster Haven and took their ease in the Ship Inn, now the Luttrell Arms, when it ceased to belong to the Abbot of Cleeve; Royalist and Parliamentarian soldiers including the great General Blake, later Admiral: Charles II when a fugitive 15-year-old prince:

packmen who frequented the Horse and Crook Inn that left its sign in the High Street, their horses carrying their goods in wooden panniers along packroads linking Exmoor, Taunton and Minehead and over packhorse bridges like Dunster's Gallox Bridge: clothiers for several centuries, who from 1680 bought yarn in the octagonal Yarn Market whither it was brought by women who had spun it from Exmoor fleeces in farmhouse, cottage and Dunster's wretched Poor House, for weavers to make into broadcloths called 'dunsters'. Up Grabbist Hill went the weavers to stretch the scoured cloths on drying-racks on the terraced slope. In 1685 three poor Sedgemoor rebels, Dunster men, passed through the streets with a crowd of onlookers to cross Gallox Bridge over the gentle rippling Avill on a September morning for hanging on Gallox Hill, where earlier lords of Dunster executed offenders. Farmers carried their corn to the Castle mills, one of which, Lower Mill, has 'clacked ever since Domesday Book' with a little interruption. Richard Jefferies described it after his visit in 1884 as 'a curious mill which has two wheels overshot, both driven by the same sluice. It was very hot . . . the mill dust sprinkled the foliage so that the leaves seemed scarce able to breathe; it dripped almost to the stream where trout were watching under a cloud of midges dancing over the ripples.' This mill has been expertly restored to working order by Mr. Arthur Capps who now leases it. Its flour can be bought and makes beautiful bread.

Even in the present century lighted lanterns carried by wassailers bobbed along the streets on a February night and into the orchards at the base of the Tor, where libations of cider were poured round the apple trees and the wassailers sang what Jefferies called 'the Somerset orchard songs'.

The Exmoor and Minehead Festival holds fine concerts in Dunster church where in the 19th century a bass-viol and two fiddlers provided the music. The church registers give vivid glimpses of Dunster history; plague burials during the Civil War; baptisms of girls with fascinating names, Armanell and Willmot, Gelyan, Thomasin and Urith; payment to the artist Richard Phelps; baptism in the 18th century of a negro, William Dunster.

The church houses a number of treasures; do not miss the wimpled alabaster Luttrell lady on her embroidered cushion nor the small sloping-topped desk with brass lock used by a Priory monk studying in the cloister. The site of the cloister-garth provides one of

St. George's, Dunster

Dunster's lovely unexpected corners, a paved sunny garden fragrant with lavender, southernwood, roses, lying north of the church and leading to the round dovecot with its conical roof, once open for the pigeons, and revolving ladder whence the Benedictines reached eggs or squabs from the niches. A little further on, the present Conduit Lane runs close to a rough track climbing to the now boarded-in stone well-house of St. Leonard's Well, source of the conduit for Priory and village. One trough for the water stood beneath the arch in the churchyard walls. At a later date this cavity was let for a shilling rent as 'ye Shoppe' where someone must have displayed a few vegetables. The 15th century Butter Cross from the High Street, on whose steps farm-wives sold eggs and butter, now stands almost unnoticed on roadside grass at Rockhead on the way to Alcombe.

Thomas Hardy set *A Laodicean,* one of his least successful novels, in Dunster. As he knew Dunster only from topographical books and maps no powerful spirit of place pervades the book as in his Dorset novels. He calls Dunster Markton, the Castle family de Stancy. Several scenes take place in the church; one between two men seated at the table in the vestry with a revolver under the baize cloth, another a love scene between the girl Paula and the architect George Somerset who is at work on alterations to the Castle.

The rather condescending young Beatrix Potter on holiday at Minehead, wrote in her Journal that Dunster was 'truly picturesque' and admitted, more warmly, that the drive from Dunster to Timberscombe was very beautiful—as it is, passing through the sylvan valley of the Avill. Her carriage passed over the old double-arched Frackford Bridge where ruins of the last fulling mill stood. Here Mrs. Alexander, the hymn-writer and wife of the Primate of Ireland, started writing 'All Things Bright and Beautiful' sung at one time by many Sunday School scholars. Perhaps Grabbist Hill, much exaggerated, was her 'purple-headed mountain' and the Avill her river running near it. Whyte-Melville stayed for a while in Dunster when writing his book, *Katerfelto,* riding to the hunt with Dunster friends.

An extrancing addition to Dunster attractions is the Doll Museum which started from Mrs. Hardwick's collection. The dolls range from a doll found in a Pharaoh's tomb to quaint or beautiful English, German and French dolls.

ELWORTHY

The name means 'Ella's clearing', after a Saxon called Ella, who felled an area of woodland and planted a settlement on this site at the eastern extremity of the Brendon Hills. Centuries before Ella, an Iron Age people—possibly the Dumnonii—constructed the hill fort, the so-called Elworthy Barrows, 1,200 feet up a mile south-west of the hamlet. Overgrown today with tangled vegetation, it was planned as a place of refuge for people with cattle in a time of invasion, and given a great circular rampart with the entrance in-turned for defence. It was never completed. Nearby runs the prehistoric trackway used by Iron Age and earlier peoples; re-used probably by Roman legionaries and Saxon soldiers, and later still by pack-trains of wool merchants travelling across the Brendons.

The russet castellated tower of St. Martin's church (now classified as 'redundant')—set in a high churchyard at the corner of a ferny lane—dates back to the 13th century, so does the lancet window in the nave, displaying two patristic figures, one with the eagle, one with the Paschal lamb. On the south wall is a framed print of Alexander Morley, Rector 1717-1731. The interior is small, with a charming screen decorated with roses and thistles and bearing the inscription, 'Lord prepare our Arts to Pray. Anno 1632.' In 1791 Collinson noted the huge yew in the churchyard, and wrote a nice description of the 'woody romantick spot' where the hamlet lay, served by rough narrow roads sunk between overhanging hedges.

About the same time a local man of means erected at considerable expense (even with cheap labour) the sham half-ruined tower called Willet Folly, that still serves as a notable landmark, a short way to the south-east. The story goes that it was built, complete with stone staircase and platform, at the request of a lady—so that she might contemplate the sweeping landscape and several aspiring church towers. The roughly paved drive for her carriage is said to lie under the grass. In 1834, in the adjoining hamlet of Willet(t), men dug into a mound in a field called 'Sparborough' and uncovered a small circle of upright stones, each about a yard high, inside which they found a cavity hollowed to contain an urn. This barrel-shaped receptacle decorated with a pattern of lines and chevrons, held burnt human bones. Barley grains on the potter's board had left their mark in his clay and helped to date the potter as a Bronze Age man.

EXFORD

Exford lies near the geographical centre of the National Park and, for many people today it is 'the capital' of Exmoor.

Certainly it was so regarded by Cecil Aldin, the artist, and Laurence Meynell, the writer, since it is 'in the hub of the Devon and Somerset hunting country', and because it has the kennels of the staghounds which, together with stables and two adjacent houses, were built in 1876 by Mardaunt Fenwick Bisset, 'the saviour of stag hunting'. Indeed it has been calculated that, farming and tourism apart, over 12 per cent of the population depends on the employment, directly or indirectly, provided by the Hunt.

Hunting lore is a vital part of Exford history, likewise some of the colourful characters connected with it. Arthur Heal was perhaps the most famous huntsman ever. He it was who permitted the Prince of Wales to adminster the death blow to the stag at bay on that memorable day in 1879 (see page 73); and it was his son, Fred, who farmed with his father at North Ley, and gave an enormous amount of information about deer and hunting to Richard Jefferies, when gathering material for his book *Red Deer* in 1883. Jefferies went walking and talking and fishing with Fred Heal, who showed him how to find deer in secluded places and inspired such fine passages as:

I see a stag. He is lying down but immediately gets up and looks straight across at me. His horns, in velvet, are as high as his ears, but his coat is in perfect condition, a beautiful red-gold colour. He is a runnable stag.

Other writers, hunting specialists apart, have described the deer and the hounds, but in his *Life in a Devon Village* Henry Williamson — when visiting the kennels — noted the 'baleful yellow fire' that could smoulder in a hound's eyes — a telling phrase.

Early this century the nature-writer W. H. Hudson, a craggy stooping man released by a small pension from city imprisonment and extreme poverty, came to explore Exmoor and began by tracing with delight the course of the River Exe, 'a silver serpent'. He followed, he said, a dream and a memory, as his forefathers (he was born in the Argentine) had dwelt beside it. So he followed the streamlet trickling out of the peat east of The Chains and down to Exford, watching brown heath change to flowery meadows and writing lyrically that on its way to Dulverton 'the Exe runs singing aloud'. He was captivated by every feature of the village: the shallow stream, the pied wagtails, the gentle, pretty faces of some of the countrywomen. He noted the numerous inns and brisk trade provided by riding and hunting. And he complained — even in 1909!—that roads near Exford were traffic-choked while whole parts of the commons were being fenced and forbidden to walkers. As Jefferies also remarked, Exmoor 'could be nibbled away'.

Not long ago a visitor entering the Methodist chapel (now converted to private use) was dazzled by the blaze of colours from two stained glass windows. Brilliant-winged angels, holding string instruments and arrayed in scarlet gowns and orange stoles, glorified their austere environment. The story is well told by Peter Hesp in *Exmoor Review 1967*. These windows were made in William Morris's workshop in 1880 to designs by Edward Burne-Jones and placed in Marylebone chapel. Years later they were acquired by the composer, Cyril Scott, who lived in Exford during the second world war and presented them to the chapel in memory of two close friends — Holland-Scott, Professor at Durham School who died at Lynmouth, and Bertram Binyon, the singer, (brother of the poet, Laurence Binyon), who is buried at Dulverton. A Porlock builder installed the windows and at the unveiling Scott wrote; 'I have very happy memories of Exford where I received many kindnesses during the troubled days of the war'. It disappointed him that Exford people took little interest in his music.

As in several other Exmoor settlements, you must climb steeply to the church, which is detached from the village proper. It is at least the third building to stand on this ancient site, close to the route of a prehistoric trackway. The dedication is to St. Salvyn, a Celtic missionary, who is represented in a stained glass window. The magnificent rood screen was imported in 1929 from a barn at West Quantoxhead, where it had lain since the church of St. Audries was demolished in 1858; otherwise the style is mainly Perpendicular, with a solid west tower, well able to stand up to the elements at nearly 1,000 feet. There is a churchyard cross, used in the last century — and probably earlier — to announce public events; while the graves or memorials include one to Jan Glass, a sheep stealer of great notoriety, and another to Robert Baker, a Good Samaritan, known to have given the clothes off his back to a passing beggar.

A number of customs have died out, but the Exford Horse Show in mid-August is an active and established event, jointly promoted by the Exmoor Pony Society — the native breed — and the Devon and Somerset Staghounds.

EXTON and BRIDGETOWN

O.S. 926337
O.S. 924333

At Heath Poult Cross there stood some years ago the Poult Inn, familiarly known as The Hare and Lady, kept by Fanny Pope who—as Jack Hurley relates in his *Legends of Exmoor,* would frequently turn herself into a hare, give the harriers their fun, and then resume her human form and her occupation of selling beer.

Fanny had a grandson who was in her confidence. He used to tell the master of hounds that he knew where they would find a hare that would give good sport. Invariably, it was Fanny who was put up; always she obliged the hunt with a splendid chase, whereupon the master would bestow a shilling upon the boy.

The system, profiting both boy and Fanny, was operated many times. The boy always ran with the harriers, and was alarmed one day when they got too close to their quarry. ' 'Urn, granny, urn, or they'll catch thee', he shouted.

But she never was caught. Almost opposite the site of the inn is the turning to Exton, two miles of road steeply falling over the green back of Exton Hill between hedges of beech where, in summer, foxgloves rise above ferns and red campions, and in places wild raspberries grow. A hedged enclosure for lambs, too small to call a field, is spread with snowdrops in February. The wind blows vigorous and cold. Some winters this road is blanketed by snow from hedge to hedge where wind-sculptured drifts pile high. In such winters Exton can become inaccessible so that the daily life of villagers and farmers is assailed by difficulties that they must and do counter with endurance and resourcefulness. Television viewers remember the documentary portraying the blizzards of 1978 and Mr. Takle of Kendle Farm, digging out scores of ewes and many dead lambs from huge drifts.

Down the hill the hamlet of Exton perches on the hill-side above the Exe Valley. The church of St. Peter, described as 'the rudest and roughest of its kind in the district' rises from a steeply sloping churchyard, swept by bracing winds. The tower is of rough stone and the interior is bare and simple. There is an old-fashioned box pew reserved for the ringers near the tower; and on the north wall a wooden plaque dated 1712, gilded and painted with an extraordinary array of skulls, skeletons, crowns, and Father Time keeps green the memory of Rose Pearse, died 1712, and of Robert who was 'joyned to his amiable spouse' twenty years later. Tablets poignantly commemorate members of the Everard family and other local families ruthlessly cut down in the two world wars. In summer

43

a jug of marguerites and foxgloves graces a table. Some years ago a gipsy funeral procession wound up the high path to the church, with a group of black-clad 'keeners' at its head, mourning and wailing.

Below the churchyard—from where you can see deer coming over Winsford Hill—stands a pretty house retaining the name 'Hare and Hounds' that it bore as the village inn before 1914. The old stable stands behind it with a long slated skittle alley and upstairs Club Room, that housed many celebrations. Here Exton farmers came to pay their rent and attend a dinner enlivened by the local brass band. Here the Friendly Society feasted after its processional walk, bearing brass-headed staves adorned with nosegays. Margaret J. Baker, well-known for her children's books, lived in this house and wrote some of her best stories here, giving them an authentic Exmoor background. For example, *Castaway Christmas* (1963) portrayed the 1960 floods, while *Cut Off from Crumpets* (1964) painted the snow scenes of the great fall of the winter of 1962-3. The present owner, Colin Wills, RIBA, is a musical craftsman who has won top national prizes for the stringed instruments he has made—'cello, violin, and viola.

In the valley below Exton lies Bridgetown, with its inn, charming riverside cricket ground, and old mill, its iron wheel silent now. When in work it was one of the largest mills on Exmoor. As described by Derrick Warren in *The Waters of Emoor:*

Its low breast wheel, 14 feet in diameter and 4 feet wide, powered three pairs of stones. In the 19th century it was owned by a well-known local family, the Phillips, one of whom, Charles, and later his son, Harry, of Cowbridge, Timberscombe, developed a businesss of 'Machinist, Wheelwright, Carpenter and Smith' . . . Their workshop was powered by a small low breast wheel in the mill tail race, and this was also used at one time to generate electricity.

The hump-backed bridge with its single arch may have given the hamlet its name. Less than a mile to the north, at Coppleham Cross, the Quarme joins the Exe, and then flow in one stream towards Blackpool, at the confluence with the Barle.

GLENTHORNE   O.S. 798497

In 1799 Robert Southey recorded that he had followed a network of paths to 'a remarkable spot, called Glenthorne, where Mr. Halliday has built a beautiful dwelling halfway up the cliff'. The Rev. W. S. Halliday, a rich and romantic clergyman was — to quote S. H. Burton's *Exmoor:*

. . . of a humorous turn of mind, one of his favourite jokes being to baffle local antiquarians by burying Roman coins in likely places over Exmoor. It was the knowledge of this trick that made them deeply suspicious of any appearance of Roman remains and, consequently, delayed positive identification of Old Barrow until recent years.

Old Barrow was the Roman fortlet built on top of the hill above Glenthorne in the first century AD to keep watch on invaders from South Wales.

With all England to choose from, Halliday fixed on this lovely impossible site to build in 1829 what was described by J. Ll. W. Page in his *An Exploration of Exmoor* as a 'pretty Tudoresque mansion'. It is sited, not 'halfway up the cliff', but in a combe or platform of ground in the side of a gorge, surrounded by woods, with a 150-foot drop to the sea. The venture was immensely difficult. Previously the tiny beach — its rocks and tides dangerous — and most of the beautiful half-savage area had been familiar mainly to smugglers and charcoal burners, who left traces of their work and half-hidden pathways between Glenthorne and Culbone to the east. No village or hamlet ever existed. Coal and supplies for the house had often to come precariously by sea, while the 3-mile zig-zag and mountainous drive down from the coast road between Porlock and Lynmouth took a year to make.

Now, bordered in summer by massed multi-coloured rhododendrons, it is the approach to the Nature Trail provided by the estate, with miles of Waymarked Walks and areas that protect wild life and rare plants and trees. The map is dotted with alluring names: Magpie Plantation, Stag's Head Wood, Sugarloaf Hill, Seven Thorns, The Pinetum; also remains of kilns, a derelict boathouse, and an ice house where blocks of ice were stored to preserve food; all created and maintained at a time when labour was plentiful and cheap.

The spring named Sisters' Fountain (after Halliday's four nieces), and crowned with a rude stone cross acquired during foreign travels, promoted the legend that Joseph of Arimathea and the young Jesus had sailed up the Bristol Channel in a trading ship which rough weather drove on to the beach at Glenthorne. Joseph and the boy walked up the combe searching for fresh water, and when they failed Christ caused a spring to rise.

The Halliday family lived for over a century in the seclusion of this oasis of peaceful beauty. Drama was provided by the sea, when a Dutch cargo ship was wrecked here in the 1880s; when a ship's name plate carved *Santa Maria* was dug up in the beach, giving rise to the belief that a Spanish Armada vessel had met her fate on the rocks; and when the headboard of the Confederate cruiser, *Alabama*, sunk off Cherbourg in 1864, came ashore. The latter is now housed in the Blake Museum, Bridgwater. Nor was the Doone connection lacking for it was at Yenworthy Farm on the estate that a widow shot one of the Doones who had fired her ricks. The flintlock that killed the marauder is still kept at Glenthorne.

On a more homely note is the anecdote attached to Oare church, which the squire and his family attended on Sundays. On one occasion they were late, and the rector absent-mindedly began the service with the familiar words, 'When the wicked man . . .' This was too much for the parish clerk, John Hancock, who called out: 'Plaze zur, he b'ant come yet.'

Yenworthy Farm, Glenthorne

Clement Kille

HAWKRIDGE

Dense woodland at the foot of Hawkridge Ridge; Tarr Steps upstream; the confluence of the Barle and the Danes Brook downstream, with Iron Age Brewer's Castle on the opposite bank and Mounsey Castle just round the corner—all this part of Exmoor has challenged the descriptive powers of several writers. '. . . a wild, picturesque country' wrote Collinson in 1791 after riding rough roads between thickets of gorse, up the steep faces of hills that looked down on uncultivated and heather-dark tracts of moor: Hawkridge at a height of 900 feet is old and often cold, looks it and feels it. To this parish belonged some of the 53 Free Suitors of the Royal Forest, described under **Withypool.** High winds sweep the ridge where a handful of houses cluster near the homely lonely church of St. Giles, with its rough square tower that defies gales and, until recently, enclosed grottoes of dank green ferns inside the walls. In such a church it is appropriate to find a stone coffin lid inscribed with Latin and Norman French in Lombardic lettering, a Norman doorway surrounded by a rustic craftsman's shaky uncertain chevron moulding, a huge rather clumsy font, decorated round its rim with rough cable ornament.

In the graveyard we read the names of families deeply rooted in this remote countryside—Sloley, Vellacott, Westcott, Bawden and Locke. The versatile skill of the Lockes, wheelwrights and carpenters, was exercised for two centuries, their handiwork ranging from coffins to gates and waggon wheels. Hunting was always deeply entrenched among clergy and laity alike. Parson John Boyse, incumbent of Hawkridge-cum-Withypool at the turn of the 18th and 19th centuries, one of the keenest stag hunters of his day, kept a laconic journal of the chase but managed, in 1805, to include at least one reference to national events:

On this day the ever memorable and glorious battle was fought off Trafalgar in which the great Lord Nelson fell.

He fairly let himself go about the hounds:

Their colour generally hare-pied, long ears, deep muzzles, large throats. In tongue they were perfect; when baying the deer they might be heard at immense distance.

Another parson, the Rev. Joseph Jekyll, who came to Hawkridge in 1833, was of a similar sort and figures in F. J. Snell's *A Book of Exmoor.* Snell tells another tale about him in his *The Blackmore Country:*

Once upon a time a villager was asked to take the place of a bass singer in the choir for one Sunday only, and consented. A day or two later he was discovered by the incumbent wading up and down the little river apparently without aim or object. The cleric drew rein and, much amazed, inquired the meaning of this extraordinary procedure. 'Plaze your honour' was the reply, 'I be trying to get a bit of a hooze on me'. In other words, he was attempting to catch a cold, so that he might become hoarse, this being, as he thought, the best means of qualifying himself for the successful discharge of his duty.

Yet another eccentric incumbent—Hawkridge seems to have bred them—was the Rev. D. S. Sweetapple-Horlock, who lived and officiated at Hawkridge 1924-47. In his day he owned Tarr Steps and, true to form, hunted with the 'D and S', walked puppies, and fished the Barle with enthusiasm. He rode regularly to church, wearing a very short cassock over his riding boots, and established at Tarr Steps Farm a small hostel for training young unemployed for farm work.

Practically every writer devotes a page or two to Ernest Bawden who, on his gravestone, is commemorated as huntsman to the Devon and Somerset Staghounds 1917-37. This man was a legend and many stories have been told of his exploits. One day a hunt lasted until the moon rose, when the stag and several hounds leaped over the cliffs near Culbone. Bawden scrambled down the cliff face and found one hound dead and three others swimming after the swimming stag. Next day the three returned to the kennels, but the stag was seen no more. Alfred Munnings, the artist, sometimes went riding with Ernest and occasionally borrowed an old horse called 'Pineapple' off him for painting excursions. Cecil Aldin, another sporting artist, made several sketches of this man. Ernest's father, James, boasted that once when ploughing on his father's farm as a boy, he heard the huntsman's horn, unharnessed the plough horse, followed the hunt for several miles riding bareback, and was in at the kill.

Hawkridge Revel is of long standing and takes place on a date near St. Giles Day, 1st September. It now incorporates a modern Gymkhana but in the past always included races between farmers, shepherds and others up and down the rough slopes of the hills. It is a little ironical that the church in this hunt-loving village should be dedicated to the saint who saved a hind from the hounds.

HEDDON'S MOUTH —
see TRENTISHOE

HOLNICOTE—see SELWORTHY

HORNER—see CLOUTSHAM

HEASLEY MILL O.S. 735323

The vivacious little river Mole has carved a valley where banks
are wooded with beech, oak and willow, making a sylvan wilderness
through which one glimpses flurrying white water. Such is the scene
above Heasley Mill hamlet. To the north, north-east and south-
east, woods on steep slopes conceal the deep shafts of old mines, the
ruins of an engine house, the sites of water wheels, and grass-
covered heaps of mining refuse. Here and there precipitous shaly
paths, streaked with the blue azurite that named Peacock Lode,
drop from hilltop to valley, made by the tipping of mining waste.
Some of the last miners in the 19th century occupied primitive stone
cottages, now disused sheds with protruding rafters, at the side of
the road leading up from the hamlet to the site of the Bampfylde
mine. Copper was mined here for centuries, on and off, reaching
right back to the Saxons who called the river the 'Yeo', one of their
favourite river names, and before that to the Celts who called it
'Nymet', meaning holy or divine : for water was life-giving and
worthy of worship—as Hazel Eardley-Wilmot pointed out in an
article on Exmoor place names in *Exmoor Review 1982.* Iron ore was
also mined in what are now farm fields within the hamlet.

In *Exmoor Review 1969* John Rottenbury gave an account of the
industry at Heasley Mill, of miners' lives, their knowledge of
mining techniques, their hard exertions that included climbing
vertical ladders, and their recreation in North Molton inns. North
Molton still has The Miners' Arms. All mining had stopped by
about 1900, but an attempt was made at revival during the last war.
The iron mine at Florence, a mile east of Heasley, was opened up
and the shaft de-watered, so that a unit of the Canadian Royal
Engineers could start work. In the *Exmoor Review 1979,* M. H. Jones
described how, when they struck some old workings, water poured
in, overwhelming the pumps, and rose within 12 feet of the top of
the shaft. The men were fortunate to escape unhurt. Later fears for
the National Park were aroused when, in 1975, the British Kynoch
Metal Company began prospecting for copper at Heasley Mill and
eastwards towards Sandyway and Kinsford Gate. The venture

however fizzled out.

Today Heasley Mill is a pretty hamlet of white and grey houses roofed with slate, a few colour-washed cottages, a little school of red-grey sandstone (now the village hall) and a Methodist chapel still in use. A rusted plough lies on the green. Beyond stands the deserted mill, its iron wheel cast out among the brambles, next to a pleasant house made from the mill's stone-walled storehouse, whose double doors gave space for lofty windows. The mill stream prattles through the garden between hart's tongue ferns, after foaming down a steep field that is the habitat of marsh marigold and water buttercup. Broadening out, splashing over stones, the Mole flows away under the other side of the lane.

Facing the mill is Forge House, and behind that lies the smithy with its black-painted half-door.

Village hall, chapel, charming guest house, witness to activity. Yet standing by the blithe little river one imagines the life that pervaded this place fifty years or more ago, when the Mole worked the mill, the anvil rang, children ran out of school, the farm horses that pulled the plough clattered to the smithy.

Kentisbury Church and Barton

Rev. W. A. Bevis

50

KENTISBURY

O.S. 623439

This is a tiny hamlet, 600 feet up on the boundary of the National Park, about 3 miles south-west of Combe Martin and 2 miles from Blackmoor Gate, once a station on the old Barnstaple-Lynton railway. It is chiefly remarkable for the fine church of St. Thomas, although the dedication is not certain. Mainly early Gothic, the building was restored and enlarged in 1875, at which date the remains of an ancient screen were removed. In his *The Buildings of England—North Devon,* Nikolaus Pevsner refers *inter alia* to the tall battlemented tower (restored in 1913), the stair turret, and a handsome sundial above the doorway in the south porch. Close by stands the Barton, incorporating a date-stone 1685. A former rector, the Rev. Thomas Openshaw, built a public elementary school in 1877 for a hundred children. To the east stands Kentisbury Down, 1106 feet, 'a roughly circular hill', with standing stones and other prehistoric remains.

LEIGHLAND

O.S. 033365

Unspoilt lanes climb up Brendon hillsides to reach Leighland, a hamlet due south of Roadwater. At times they follow the course of streams that encourage ferns and primroses to grow luxuriantly under the beeches and ash trees. Outside the hamlet Stamborough Farm stands high, overlooking valley pastures and the outskirts of open Exmoor. The artist, John William North, spent his last years in this old farmhouse and died there in 1924. He sketched stone barns and those of Little Stamborough Farm across the lane. Not far away he painted his *Exmoor Ponies.* If his sketch, *Landscape with Chapel,* was made here, it transfigured the very plain Victorian church in its setting of woods and fields, that in 1862 had replaced an ancient and attractive chapel, of which photographs still exist: both lay within the ecclesiastical parish of Old Cleeve. The dedication to St. Giles, always depicted with the deer (or hind) associated with his miracles, remains appropriate to the district where deer still roam. A panel painted with the figure of St. Giles in his abbot's gown, his hind at his feet, stands at the west end of the church, the work of Rachel Reckitt, of Golsoncott. In the late 18th century the vicar was Coleridge's acquaintance, the Rev. James Newton, who gave hospitality to Mrs. Coleridge and her infant son.

Leigh Barton Chapel—West End

In the early 19th century a band of rustic musicians, who occupied the old chapel's west gallery, became locally famous, like those of Hardy's Mellstock. In his *Carols of West Somerset,* Dr. Glyn Court tells how instrumentalists were led by a remarkable Leighland man, by the name of George Matthews, who worked at Pitt Mill Farm and had a passion for music, passing his evenings in 'pricking out' the notation of old carols, anthems, psalms, for church use and of songs and dances for local revels. He also composed original tunes for this little orchestra which he trained with strict discipline: fiddles, clarinets, trombone, flute, and serpent. The group was in great demand.

A mile to the south-west of Leighland stands Leigh Barton on a lofty site at the top of a steep and shady lane. The house is a sturdy stone building, with a pleasing facade given grace by a pilastered porch of Ham stone. Stone barns and an ancient horse mill lie alongside. This was the home for many years of the Poyntz family who, in the 16th century, owned lands at Dunster. In 1583 Edward Poyntz was buried in the north aisle of Dunster church beneath a stone that had once been an altar slab. By the time of the Commonwealth his grandson Giles was in serious trouble as a 'delinquent' Catholic gentleman, who refused to relinquish his faith and religious practices. At secluded Leigh Barton the family felt tolerably secure and for 22 years maintained their household chaplain, Dom Philip Powel, a Welsh monk from Douai who had been ordained priest. At Leigh Barton he said Mass in a chapel later used as a barn. Fellow Catholics from around Exmoor worshipped there. During the Civil War he spent six months with the Royalist army under General Goring. After its dispersal, he took passage in a boat to Wales but was captured by a Parliamentarian party that came aboard. In 1646 he was sentenced to a dreadful death at Tyburn and dragged to it on a hurdle, protesting to the end that he had committed no crime. 'I am a monk of this Holy Order'. The corporal or cloth that he used at Mass before execution came into possession of Downside Abbey; and an account of his life and martyrdom was published in the *Downside Review* in 1893.

In June, on the anniversary of his execution, a service in memory of Father Powel is celebrated by the Rector of Old Cleeve and attended by members of his congregations in the chapel that has served as a barn. One local legend holds that Father Powel's ghost haunts Leigh Woods on the date of his death, and that a man lost his wits on seeing a gory apparition there. The story is based on the belief that the body was returned to Leigh Barton and immured behind the south wall of the chapel. In fact it was buried at Moorfields.

LUCCOMBE   *O.S. 910445*

This tiny village lies less than a mile from Horner, sandwiched between Horner Hill and Knowle Top. Whether the name means 'enclosed valley' or 'lovers' valley' is immaterial, as its seclusion and charm suit both derivations. So diminutive, so pretty, it resembles a young child's picture-book village. Yet the sandstone and cream-washed walls under their cosy thatch or bark-brown tiles reflect robustness and endurance, evidence of the skill of masons and thatchers who knew how to handle local materials to best advantage.

The houses—different in design and detail, while composing a charming pattern of colour and texture—line the main street and run up Stoney Street, round a corner near the church. One cottage bears the date 1680 over the door. The only shop is the toylike post office, with its overhanging thatch and half-door. The stream fringed with yellow loosetrife and hart's tongue fern flows under trees at the roadside, breaking at intervals into little waterfalls.

No school or inn, but a magnificent church of St. Mary, 13th century in origin, with a west tower 82 feet high, and an interior full of light, thanks to whitewashed walls and lancet windows. There are many things of merit to look for: fragments of golden medieval glass in the east window of the south aisle, recovered from Selworthy after drastic restoration in 1840; carved foliage on the capitals of the pillars; carved bosses painted and gilded in the roof; a two-foot long brass in front of the chancel step, depicting a man wearing a gown and starched ruff—'William Harrison . . . who fell asleep . . . in the year of Our Lord 1615'. But the principal memorial is on the north wall, inscribed with a Latin epitaph and surmounted by a coat-of-arms set with jewel-like pieces of coloured glass. It enshrines a story of Civil War adventure, courage and tragedy—that of Dr. Henry Byam, vicar of Luccombe and Selworthy and a staunch Royalist. Cromwellian soldiers seized him. His wife and daughter were drowned when trying to escape across the Bristol Channel with their servants. Byam himself escaped with his sons to join Charles I; and, after the king's execution, escaped again to the Scillies with young Prince Charles, finally to be restored to his Luccombe parish, dying there in 1669 at the age of 89.

On the south wall there is a tablet to E. W. Hendy, the Exmoor naturalist and writer. The inscription speaks for him:

Because he so loved the beauty of this church and its surroundings, this tablet is placed here
in memory of
ERNEST WILLIAM HENDY
of Porlock
who loved, watched and wrote about birds and saw all natural beauty as a manifestation of
God.

The church is well loved. Members of St. Albans Cathedral choir sing Eucharist and Evensong at the end of July. They camp for several days at a Luccombe Farm. The family of a former Dean of St. Albans presented the carved Jacobean chair seen in the sanctuary of the church.

Eleanor Helme, the children's writer, who set her stories in Exmoor (several illustrated by Lionel Edwards), lived at Luccombe. Another very different writer, W. J. Turner, wrote an analytical account of the village based on factual investigation by Mass Observation, a book beautifully illustrated in colour and black and white. Rarely has any village—on Exmoor or anywhere else—been so minutely dissected!

A very different concept is projected by Samuel Palmer's painting, *Coming Out of Evening Church,* in which church, stream and congregation are seen in moonlight, bearing a conjectural resemblance to Luccombe.

LUCKWELL BRIDGE   *O.S. 905387*

Motorists speeding along the road from Wheddon Cross often miss Luckwell Bridge, as most of it lies just off their route. On a fine day it is a pleasure to stroll round this half-hidden hamlet, this valley of the tumbling, babbling Quarme and its numerous rivulets, this region of welling springs that have given their name to farms like Hawkwell and Honeywell.

The bridge itself is of rough red sandstone tufted with moss. Near it the Quarme stream broadens, and overhanging trees make green reflections in the water. Riders let their horses drink here, and sometimes an old white horse stands in the shallows. Turning left, the Quarme becomes noisier as it runs over stones and boulders and falls into a cascade. Here it used to form the mill stream. The mill has ceased working, but the house remains. Trout swim in the stream and at times herons stand fishing.

To the right of the bridge is a wall with a broken sandstone arch and the old pipe of a pump—nothing at all picturesque — and here, in a field just behind the wall, covered for the sake of safety by a rough heap of stones, is the source of the hamlet's name: St. Luke's Well, once a healing well, named after Luke the Physician.

Luckwell Bridge is in the parish of Cutcombe. In the 19th and early 20th centuries an energetic Nonconformism (Bible Christian, then Methodist) flourished in the hamlet and drew members of the farming community to chapel. Congregations were known to number as many as 100, and there were vigorous assemblies. In his *Methodists in West Somerset,* A. G. Pointon states:

A popular arrangement for the Circuit Rally was a tea at Luckwell Bridge combined with a pilgrimage of witness to Dunkery Beacon, 2½ steep miles away, and a meeting on the slopes.

The first chapel is built into Steppes Cottage. The second, erected in 1884, is the white slate-roofed building now standing deserted near the bridge—there are plans to convert it into a dwelling—a sad little page of rural history.

Apart from the mill house and another house near the bridge that was once a village shop, there is a house on the higher main road called The Old Inn, dating perhaps from coaching days. Yet another cottage is remembered as a sweetshop; and a pretty place, with white walls set off by a wealth of geraniums and petunias, is called The Old Forge. Older people still remember cottages and craftsmen of rich and eccentric character living in this 'little hamlet, musical of rills' as the Rev. Lewis Court called it in verses that depict it as:

> A dozen cottage roof-trees grouped around
> A modest chapel by a silver brook.

LUXBOROUGH   *O.S. 974380*

The pattern of this village has scarcely changed for centuries, as a recent survey undertaken by Edward F. Williams for the Somerset Archaeological and Natural History Society makes plain. There is no single village centre, but three hamlets, and a scatter of farms with small enclosed fields. On the hilltop, due south of Croydon Hill, is 'churchtown', comprising St. Mary's church and several dwellings that formerly included the Luxborough (earlier Lethbridge) Arms inn, the school house, and until 1971 a village school described by Cicely Cooper in her *Memoirs of Selworthy,* in which she remembers pupils who walked several miles to school from outlying farms and hamlets. 'Merry streams', as Collinson, the historian, called them, tumble down between the hills to reach kingsbridge and Pooltown at the bottom of the parish. Here are neat cottages, a post office and shop, a chapel, and the Royal Oak Inn where, for many years the instrument called 'the serpent', played in St. Mary's church by a former innkeeper, hung over the fireplace.

Collinson tells us that one 'merry stream' flowed through combe and meadows to feed a 'chain of ponds, with swarms of trout and sometimes a swan'. Later these trout ponds adorned the grounds of Chargot House built by Sir Thomas Lethbridge on Saxon foundations in 1827, and acquired by another historic family, the Malets, in 1926. In the *Exmoor Review 1979,* Sir Edward Malet painted a graphic picture of local life in the 1920s and early 1930s:

Cottage at Kingsbridge, Luxborough

V.B.C.

describing farms where horses pulled wagons and putts; the sawmill under a chestnut, the smithy, the carpenter's shop, the carter, the baker, the village nurse. Characters were unforgettable, Mary Cording, for instance:

For her cottage, she paid half-a-crown yearly and came to present the half-crown personally—this was quite a ceremony; she handed over her coin to my father, who gave it back to her with a glass of port and they had a long chat . . . On one occasion my mother asked, 'Mary, have you ever had an old age pension'? 'No, my lady, because I don't know rightly how old I be', she replied. My mother, who knew she was a good Christian, asked her if she had a Bible. 'That I have', she replied, 'but I can never read 'un' . . . sure enough on the flyleaf there were Mary's antecedents with their dates of birth, faithfully recorded, including Mary herself. My mother told her, 'I believe you are 88, Mary'. She got her pension.

Other anecdotes, e.g. those about Jan and Nathan Palmer of Luxborough, two sturdy eccentrics, will be found in an article by Dr. Glyn Court in the *Exmoor Review 1984*.

Naturally all this has changed. The old self-sufficient society has disappeared. Farming has converted much moor and scrub to good pasture; and the Forestry Commission has planted square miles of conifers on the hills round Luxborough. The old coach drive from Chargot to Brendon Hill—'a fairyland in 1926, carpeted with grass, lined with staghorn and sphagnum moss, crowned with rhododendrons and a background of well-grown beech and oak' is now a metalled road lined with conifers. Wild creatures like woodcock, heath poult, most wood-loving birds, and the little red squirrel have gone. On the other hand the choked and derelict trout pools at Chargot have recently been cleared and their stonework repaired by young workers from the British Conservation Trust.

Few signs now remain of the once vigorous and briefly prosperous mining of iron ore, developed in the 19th century on Brendon Hill. The story is told by R. J. Sellick in two books on the subject (see *Book List*). A start had been made in 1839 in Chargot Wood by Sir Thomas Lethbridge, and the first mine proper, Lothbrook, was exploited in the 1840s outside the parish at Withiel Hill. Other mines, within the parish, and opened later were Langham Hill, Beerland Wood and Kennisham Hill. At the latter the engine house and chimney were demolished by the Forestry Commission in 1978 and all that can be seen now is a clearing in the softwood forest.

In the churchyard at St. Mary's there are stone and slate tombstones, some with worn coats of arms, including those to members of the Malet family. Another dated 1888 reads 'Hier Lyeth the Body of Elisabeth Parmer'. The former schoolhouse is now a house called 'Palmer's Castle'. The saddleback tower with slate roof is a striking feature, and contains a peal of five bells. Although heavily restored in the 19th century, the interior is attractive and retains some ancient features. The church is served by the incumbent of Cutcombe, where the living at one time was held by three generations of the Jenoure family. The village school is now a pretty sandstone house called 'Plaisance', and the old inn has become 'Rosebank'. The fine wrought iron gates are the work of a local craftsman, Harry Horrobin, of Roadwater. Was the stone basin by the gate, which catches the clear water running from the spring in the high field, ever a holy well?

A woodland path beyond the gate leads, by difficult access, to the site of Clicket, a deserted village. Here are the remains of Thorn Farm and its old walnut, the ruined mill with dry leat and weed-choked stream, broken mill stones, cottage walls and residues of bread ovens, old beams lying under the scrub oaks. An evicted couple once lived in the windowless mill. Now one listens for a footstep, a voice. The site can also be approached from Timberscombe (see p.95).

LYNCH—see BOSSINGTON

The Harbour at Lynmouth

Rev. W. A. Bevis

LYNMOUTH and   *O.S. 725495*
LYNTON   *O.S. 720495*

Lynton and Lynmouth were little known to the rest of the world until the second half of the 18th century. Lynmouth had been, like other places along the coast, a small port importing coal, culm and limestone, exporting livestock and other produce of the hinterland, and for a time it had been busy with herring fishing and curing. This industry seems to have died out by about 1800, a date that coincides with the beginnings of the tourist trade, itself engendered by the cult of the picturesque. Even so, communications remained poor, so that—if they did not arrive by boat—most visitors still had to arrive on horseback or on foot.

Thus, in the summer of 1798, young Hazlitt walked from Nether Stowey with Coleridge (aged 26) and his friend John Chester, banging on an inn door after dark to be served bacon and eggs. At breakfast they looked out on a sunny garden where hives that had supplied their honey stood among thyme and flowers. They roamed the sands, picked up seaweeds, heard the tale of a fisher boy's drowning. Here in a thunderstorm Coleridge ran about the Valley

59

of the Rocks to enjoy 'the commotion of the elements' in the weird, wild hollow which, in *Lorna Doone,* R. D. Blackmore would make the abode of Mother Meldrum 'gathering sticks and brown fern'. Coleridge and Wordsworth thought of using it as the setting of a poem, *The Wanderings of Cain.* Both Wordsworth and his sister, Dorothy, who called it the 'Valley of Stones' in her letters, came several times. All of them took the route that T. E. Brown, the Victorian poet ('A garden is a lovesome thing, God wot!') remembered in his *Lynton Verses* — the beautiful zigzag coastal path from Porlock that ran alongside moorland coloured by blues, greens and 'browns where the crimson dwells'.

Robert Southey described the 'Valley' with sombre eloquence: 'the palace of pre-Adamite kings', 'the very bones and skeleton of the earth'. He climbed Duty Point, and admired the 'rude portal' of Castle Rock. Of Lynmouth he wrote that, apart from Cintra, it was 'the finest spot that I ever saw', and that its roads were 'of serpentining perpendicularity', inaccessible to carriages.

Seventeen-year-old Harriet Shelley adored Lynmouth when she arrived with Shelley (aged 20) on honeymoon in June 1812. As if in a dream she looked at the tiny white cottages, the fishing boats, the small blue bay, the climbing street, the trees, the flowers growing so profusely in the gentle climate. 'We have roses and myrtles, the house is thatched, such a little place it seems more like a fairy scene'. Haulage of Shelley's trunks, full of books, up steep Mars Hill (as it is called now) proved a problem. They were happy for a while in their cottage (the exact location is not certain), taking long walks, watching the packhorses labouring along the path to Porlock with panniers of lime and fish, hearing tales of smugglers who used the harbour. In the Valley of the Rocks Shelley scrawled tiny sketches of the fantastic rock shapes on the backs of his letters—so said his friend, Hogg—and observed that 'All shows of sky and earth, of sea and valley, are here'. By the autumn however he wanted more society. Moreover he had earned local hostility by such incomprehensible actions as the throwing of matchwood boats and green bottles containing propaganda leaflets into the sea. But all that summer he had worked at his long poem, *Queen Mab,* that opens as if prophetically:

> How wonderful is Death,
> Death and his brother Sleep.

Charles Kingsley came to Lynmouth in 1849 with his wife and

Lynton Cliff Railway

Rev. W. A. Bevis

two children. Here he built up his health and happiness after a period of illness and dark depression, walking, collecting sea plants and shells in the company of Froude, the future eminent historian, who became his brother-in-law. R. D. Blackmore came to Lynton in the 1860s to gather material for *Lorna Doone*: followed in 1873 by Francis Kilvert, curate and diarist, who wrote of the scenery with his usual spontaneity, viewing it in morning light:

Glowing with all its superb colouring . . . the red cliffs . . . purple heather slopes . . . the rich brown wilderness of rustling fern . . . the snowy foam fringe chafing the feet of the cliffs.

These travellers found the place relatively unfrequented, its buildings mostly cob cottages. Indeed when Henry James praised Lynton's beauty, he feared to attract a wider public; but watching the approach of evening from the summit of Castle Rock, the sea-mews crying around him, he called one of 'the charmed moments of English travel'. Much later, in her book, *The Tamarisk Tree*, Dora Russell described staying at the Valley of Rocks Hotel in the winter of 1924, when she and Bertrand, in a room 'high up' with a view 'over grey rocks, sky and the warm brown wet bracken' sat by the fire contentedly reading and writing: she *Hypatia*, he *What I believe*. In 1926 they spent 'a wonderful communal Christmas' at the hotel with Meynells, Stracheys, Joads, children and a nurse. Joad disliked the children who 'rampaged with their toys'.

61

In St. Mary's church, Lynton—much rebuilt over the past 200 years—there is a monument to Hugh Wichehalse who died in 1653, and whose family were lords-of-the-manor of Lynton 1560-1713. From 1628 he lived at Ley, now Lee Abbey, an ugly building built on the site of the old farmhouse, called Ley Manor in *Lorna Doone*. Jan Ridd was hospitably entertained there by the Wichehalses who succeeded those doomed members of the family whose legend Blackmore recounted with embelishments in *Tales from the Telling House*. Never an abbey, Lee is now a Christian conference centre.

The man most responsible for developing and popularising both Lynton and Lynmouth some 90 years ago was the publisher, Sir George Newnes, who lived at Hollerday House (destroyed by fire in 1913 engineered, it is said, by suffragettes) and presented Lynton with its florid Town Hall. Newnes also backed the building of the cliff railway, conceived and completed in 1890 by a local man of genius, Bob Jones, whose family operate it to this day. He was also behind the construction of the narrow gauge line from Barnstaple to Lynton, opened in 1898 and closed for lack of business in 1935.

Lynton, it must be admitted, is undistinguished architecturally, but—the Town Hall apart—it does possess two institutions of interest. One is the Convent of the Poor Clares in Lee Lane, built in 1909 for exiled nuns from France. Here a small community of brown-habited Sisters pass their lives in poverty and prayer. The Convent Church of the Most Holy Saviour—it serves the public— has a High Altar of veined blue-green marble from an Orsini chapel in Rome. It contains a casket holding relics of four Roman martyrs taken from the catacombs. The other place of interest is the charming little Exmoor Museum housing bygones in St. Vincent's Cottage, displaying tools and products of former craftsmen such as the blacksmith, turf-cutter, trapper, candle maker.

Lynmouth, visually attractive, has more than one niche in local history. One was the famous incident when, on a wild January night in 1899, the lifeboat was hauled up Countisbury Hill and taken 13 miles overland to Porlock to stand by a ship in distress. The other was the devastating flood that overwhelmed the town on 16 August 1952, following a lengthy period of rain and a cloudburst on The Chains high up on Exmoor. Both these events are described in a number of books and articles, but a clear and concise account can be found in Jack Hurley's *Snow and Storm on Exmoor*. And there is a powerful fictional account of the flood in Henry Williamson's *The Gale of the World*.

MALMSMEAD   O.S. 791477

The place is known to thousands who come to see the house where they believe Jan Ridd brought his bride Lorna, now called Lorna Doone Farm. The scene is idyllic; the white house roofed with red tiles; the whitewashed stables full of ponies with young riders round the door; the glistening shallows of the ford; the old bridge arching over rippling Badgworthy Water as it runs into the Lyn. Close at hand lie the combes that Blackmore explored and exploited with such love and freedom: the sylvan Badgworthy Valley; Hoccombe Combe, where he saw fragments of ruined walls; Lank Combe with its long pale water-slide—all impregnated with Doone legend, all lovely to explore and linger in.

'An adventure which influenced my whole life' wrote Llewelyn Powys of his visit to Malmsmead, described in the chapter on Exmoor, in his book *Somerset and Dorset Essays*. As a schoolboy from Montacute Vicarage he and his brother Littleton travelled by train to Minehead, where a farmcart took them to stay a few days on Malmsmead Farm.

We reached the farm at twilight. While our evening meal was preparing I had time to run out and stand on the bridge to watch the trout poised in the clean water below. Day and night the sound of the river was audible in John Ridd's farm . . . when I waked in the small hours, curled up beside my brother on a huge feather bed, I would hear it still . . . It was as though we lay during those nights dreaming in the bowl of a huge silver bell.

We set out up Badgery Water on a morning of sunshine, our pockets stuffed with provisions. Side by side we walked over wide stretches of burned heather, the charred, twisted, twigs of which kept loosening the laces of my boots. In after years when I rode across land in Africa devastated by a bush fire it was always to the fells around Dunkery Beacon that my dreams would go.

Lorna Doone Farm, Malmsmead

S. H. Burton

MARTINHOE and WOODY BAY

Happy all, who timely know
The bright gorge that lies below
Trentishoe and Martinhoe

wrote the poet Lionel Johnson in 1888 after looking down from these tiny twin villages. Saxon Matta settled his folk at Martinhoe where Roman legionaries had manned a fort in the first century A.D. and lived in wooden huts. Torn by Atlantic winds Martinhoe sits high on the green and russet moors, looking, as J.H.B. Peel wrote, 'over a green carpet of pasture and a blue carpet of the sea', surveying the promontories of a jagged coastline that sweeps from Woody Bay to the Valley of the Rocks. A tortuous lane or a dizzy cliff path will bring you down to the shore and within sight of the caves at the foot of the cliffs haunted by screaming seabirds. The blue sea can become a green-grey monster thundering into the caves' passages. Here the Hollow Brook plunges over a cliff. In *Exmoor* S. H. Burton writes:

> The stream rises near Martinhoe and falls to sea level in just over half a mile, its average gradient being about one in four. Between the road and the cliff there is a series of falls, the finest tumbling into a deep chine. Then, below the track, the Hollow Brook disappears over the cliff and leaps 200 feet to the beach, there entering a narrow boulder-piled gulley through which it passes to the sea. The first part of this lower and most spectacular fall—which can be seen only from a boat—consists of two cascades which unite half-way down.

In all probability this part of the coast inspired some of the scenery in Henry Kingsley's *Ravenhoe* (1861), to which Cicely Cooper referred, in *Exmoor Review 1974,* when she set out with friends to find some of the places described.

In the 1870s young James Hannington, later curate at Martinhoe and Trentishoe, nearly drowned in one of the sea caves. He was rusticated from Oxford for coaching by the rector at Martinhoe; but he frequently forsook his studies to explore, on foot or on his bold-hearted pony, the precipitous tracks, cliffs, caves and strand. He adored the wildness of the place, and the Scriven boys at the rectory loved to share some of his dangerous forays. The tale is well told by A. Hunter in *Exmoor Review 1973.* As curate Hannington became a beloved eccentric wearing yellow cord breeches and nailed boots, riding round the parish with Bible and medical remedies. Parishioners imparted their own folk cures and beliefs, such as the certainty that ghosts walked the churchyard at Midsummer Eve. At

Martinhoe Church

Martinhoe he enjoyed feasting and revelry at Christmas, New Year, skating parties, weddings and, not least, funerals where the inhabitants were regaled on roast beef, cider, puddings and cream. In due course Hannington became the first Bishop of Eastern Equatorial Africa, but was murdered in Uganda. Today the Hannington Hall is used for meetings and social events. The rectory has become a hotel; earlier, an incumbent found a medieval font cast away in the garden and gave it to Parracombe.

In June 1914 H. W. Boon, then a 16-year-old schoolboy spent a holiday at Martinhoe. Writing in the *Exmoor Review 1979,* he described how, after a lengthy journey to Barnstaple Town station, he picked up the 'quaint curtained old narrow-gauge train'.

I was thrilled to note that the train climbed from about sea level to 1,000 feet at Woody Bay station. Here we alighted to feel the freshness of the high moorland air. Farmer Ridd, of Martinhoe, had sent a contraption known as the 'long-tailed cart' to meet us.

Boon was staying with the Delbridge family at Ivy Cottage, close to the church. Noticing his interest in butterflies and moths, Mr. Delbridge told him that in the 1880s the naturalist-writer, Richard South, had taken him—when a boy—out on the cliffs to observe by lantern light nightfeeding larvae of rare moths.

During the second world war Malcolm Elwin, the critic, biographer of Charles Reade and Llewelyn Powys, and authority on Byron, lived here with his family in a small bungalow a thousand feet up above Woody Bay. Woody, by the way, is an incorrect rendering of Wooda Bay, the scene, as Grahame Farr tells us in his *Ships and Harbours of Exmoor* of an attempt by Colonel Benjamin Lake of Martinhoe Manor to develop the locality as a holiday resort. In 1889 Squire Lake obtained an Order authorising him to build a pier about 100 yards long and a public approach road. Work however on a modified scheme did not start until 1895, and the first steamer called in 1897. Misfortunes then followed fast, gales virtually demolished the pier and in 1902 the wreckage had to be removed. 'A deliverance' was the general opinion, and confirmed when the National Trust gained possession of the area in 1965.

The church, extensively restored shortly before Hannington's arrival, has several tablets to the Blackmore family. One inscribed to Margaret Whichehalse, who married yeoman Richard Blackmore in 1683, reminds us that the author of *Lorna Doone* traced his descent from this man. It was at Martinhoe that he collected the story of the villainous Doone who entered a farmhouse where a mother, hiding in terror, saw him kill a baby by tossing it high in the air as he chanted:

> If any man asketh who killed thee
> Say 'twas the Doones of Bagworthy.

MONKSILVER   *O.S. 073374*

'Monk' derives from connections with Goldcliff Priory in Monmouthshire, while 'silver' was the original name of the stream that shaped the sinuous curves of this valley and, joined by others further north, falls into the sea at Doniford. Monksilver, a very pretty village, draws its attractions from the stream, the pleasant juxtaposition of colour-washed houses and cottages, kept in excellent order, the Notley Arms and its magnificent 19th century barn, once the coach house of an older inn, now a private dwelling called Half Moon cottage—and all this set against a background of groves of poplars, hedgebanks bright with borage and foxgloves, emerald green pastures and red soil.

The church of All Saints stands on higher ground to the west of the village street and is the repository of both beauty and interest: carved bench ends portraying the Green Man, quaint fish, antlered

Notley Arms Barn, Monksilver

stag; one of Somerset's two wooden eagle-lecterns; an Easter Sepulchre still in use. The story goes that the south aisle was built in the 16th century from funds provided by a local blacksmith who had chanced upon a sackful of gold; and that implements of his trade were incorporated in the stained glass of a 'blacksmith's window'. This is false for, as in many other churches, the glass at Monksilver displays emblems of the Passion, the work in this instance of John Toms, a mid-19th century craftsman of Wellington. In the churchyard planted with rose trees, there are graves of the Notley family, who once owned Combe Sydenham (see below). Moon daisies sometimes bloom around the stone cross. The ragged dark yew, planted by another blacksmith in 1770, casts shadows on the red path and overhangs two lichened grave stones, whose inscriptions catch the eye. One commemorates aged Mrs Elizabeth Conibeer and her two middle-aged daughters, all found brutally murdered in 1775 in the hamlet of Woodford nearby. It is startling to read an epitaph addressed to a murderer: 'Inhuman wretch! Where'er thou art—'. The event is recorded in Jack Hurley's *Murder and Mystery on Exmoor*. The other tombstone might have interested Thomas Hardy as it is inscribed 'To the memory of John Hole, aged 72, Chorister in this church for 62 years'.

In 1880 Richard Jefferies came to Monksilver, roving solitary alongside the stream, making notes for his book, climbing the hill slopes to trout pools and oakwoods full of game, and talking to poachers, who confided to him some of their artful tricks. The hand of death was already laid on this great writer, but his Exmoor visit gave him a respite. Out of it came his book, *Red Deer,* in which the chapter 'A Manor House in Deer Land' beautifully describes the Monksilver valley and the Tudor manor house of Combe Sydenham close by. The present structure was erected on medieval foundations by Sir George Sydenham in 1580. One wing and three of the four original towers were probably demolished during the Civil War, before partial rebuilding after the Restoration in 1660. The jumble of red walls and roofs, the remaining single tower, are visible from the roadside; but visitors may now see over the Hall, inspect some of the outbuildings and grounds, with the restored and restocked trout pools and the newly made herb garden, and spend the best part of the day in the deer park and tramping the woodland walks. See picture on p.119.

Here too there is a legend recorded in several books, notably by Jack Hurley in *Legends of Exmoor.* Briefly, the heiress Elizabeth Sydenham was betrothed to Sir Francis Drake, who then departed on a long voyage. In his absence she accepted another suitor and set out to marry him in Stogumber church. At the critical moment, however, an enchanted cannonball, fired across the world, crashed from the sky, landed on the train of her gown and sent her home to await Drake's return. She married him as his second wife in 1585. The cannonball (a meteorite?) was seen by Jefferies and earlier by Robert Southey who observed: 'It has been used as a weight upon the harrow of the farm; if removed it returns to the estate'. For a while it was placed in the County Museum at Taunton, but subsequent owners brought it back and it can be seen in the Hall today.

NETTLECOMBE   O.S. 056378

This is a small village, part of the benefice of Monksilver, with two or three cottages and several farms; also the house at Huish Barton, an early example of the use of bricks in Somerset and notable for its 17th century plasterwork. But the pride of the place is Nettlecombe Court, the great family house and estate of the Trevelyan family, now a centre for Field Studies, run by the Leonard Wills Trust and providing courses and excursions for the study of ecology of this rewarding countryside.

Trevelyans owned Nettlecombe for about 500 years following 300 years' possession by the Raleighs with whom they were united in marriage. A Tudor John Trevelyan built the main structure of the Court, improved and extended four generations later by another John—retaining the late-medieval range of buildings that included the kitchen. At the Somerset Record Office you may handle the domestic account books of the 18th century housekeeper whose recipes included 'sparrowgrass soup' and 'apel pudding'. Trevelyans came from Cornwall—or, by legend, from the Land of Lyonesse that broke away from the mainland in a storm and sank beneath the sea. A Trevelyan was saved by his horse that carried him back to the Cornish shore, so that the 'swimming horse' became the family badge. Its image rears proudly from the stone gateposts of the Court and swims amid waves in the rich plasterwork of a ceiling, surrounded by swags of fruit and flowers and cherubs, with which later Trevelyans had their great rooms and hall decorated.

Almost every object in the time-weathered church, adjoining the Court, is a link with distant centuries. Sculptures on the font carved in 1470 illustrate the Seven Sacraments—the ladies' horned headdresses may be similar to that worn by Alice Chaucer (daughter-in-law of the poet), the donor. In dim tomb recesses repose yellow Ham stone effigies of crusading and medieval knights: Sir Simon Raleigh with sword and shield; Sir John Raleigh, a giant of 7 feet, with dog at foot, his lady by his side, with flowing whimple and her own whippet.

In the Trevelyan Chapel Keatsian colours, ultramarine, gold, crimson, amethyst, are cast on the floor by stained glass windows of which one displays the swimming horse. Among the gorgeously arrayed saints in the windows is little-known St. Urith sheltering a child in her cloak and carrying a scythe. She was one of several saints murdered by haymakers. A niche holds a bronze sculpture of a Mother and Child, set there in memory of 'Joan Alys Wolseley, Dear Child and Heiress of Sir Walter Trevelyan of Nettlecombe'. The unique treasure of this church is rarely seen—an exquisite paten and chalice with ornamented knop, the oldest examples (c.1469) in England of work date-marked by the Goldsmiths' Company. It is now kept at St. Nicholas' Museum in Bristol, but used at Nettlecombe's patronal festival.

During the Civil War the Royalist Trevelyans suffered

persecution and destruction of property. Buildings were burned and horses seized after the head of the family had been imprisoned. Legend has it that his dauntless wife hid the family silver, and then had oxen harnessed to her coach for the long journey to London where, after long delay, she ransomed her husband. She died of smallpox on the way back. In the 18th century a Nettlecombe maid dropped her thimble through a fissure in the floorboards. When the board was taken up, a hoard of Tudor cups and other silver was revealed, including the communion plate. In the following century the Sir John Trevelyan of the day sent home at the last minute the men who came to fell a number of splendid oaks, for which he had been offered £30,000 by the shipbuilders. His heart failed him as these trees had been there as long as the Trevelyans.

Raleigh Trevelyan's book, *A Pre-Raphaelite Circle* (1979), portrays Pauline Trevelyan, wife of Sir John and friend of Ruskin's circle, one of whom described Nettlecombe as follows:

> This place is one of the most lovely I have ever seen. An Elizabethan mansion in a hollow of emerald green park with hundreds of fallow deer and the finest oaks, ashes, cedars in England. Magnolia trees . . . with white lily-shaped flowers as large as one's head.

Pauline's head is sculptured in plaster on the staircase wall.

The artist, John William North lived at Beggearnhuish House nearby, and is buried in the 'new' graveyard at Nettlecombe. A close friend of Richard Jefferies, the writer and naturalist, he gave hospitality to Jefferies' widow and son.

Meet at Nettlecombe Court

H. H. Hole

70

Oare Church and Congregation

Rev. W. A. Bevis

OARE   *O.S. 802473*

As numerous as pilgrims to the shrine of a saint, visitors flock to the diminutive square-towered church where Lorna, in her white wedding dress 'clouded with faint lavender', was shot by Carver Doone standing outside the one-light south window. Here they see the memorial to Lorna's talented creator in the form of a medallion portrait with the inscription:

To the Memory
of Richard Doddridge Blackmore
died 1900

Many, however, are drawn to Oare itself—'a parish of woods and moors' as Jan Ridd called it. It is sought by artists, naturalists, campers, riders, walkers, not in droves but in twos and threes, and now houses a hut used by the Exmoor Natural History Society as its Field Centre. The Society holds its annual service in Oare Church. Here is authentic Exmoor. 'You are in a new land, and what a land it is.' E. W. Hendy wrote about Oare country in *Wild Exmoor through the Year*. 'Mile after mile . . . of rolling moorland, in August

71

incarnadined with purple ling'.

It is a land of lovely streams: Badgworthy Water, East Lyn watering the meadows, Weir Water running between rocks and ferns, limpid Chalk Water and Oare Water whose Celtic river-name may have attached itself to the settlement. Autumn turns these moors to red-gold; the deer are roused from the coppery woods; this is the very home of the Hunt. When the autumn moon rises, the belling of rutting stags echoes from the combes. In his *Exmoor Sporting and Otherwise,* the Rev. A. J. Marshall related how, one August day, he and his wife saw the antlered heads of twenty-two stags cross the brow of a hill 'like a moving forest'. Hunting continues when the moor is rimed with frost, adding traditional colour and animation to the landscape. Late winter brings nights of howling blackness when some people, Jan Ridd among them, have thought to hear weird voices calling across the moor. A number of winters have brought Arctic snowfall, In 1963, for instance, whole communities were cut off for weeks at a time. In his *Snow and Storm on Exmoor,* Jack Hurley recorded:

The clatter of helicopters over moor and hill was now a daily sound. Food was dropped for 1,000 hungry sheep on Brendon Common . . . At Cloud Farm, Oare, Farmer Bob Nancekivell was needing insulin. His son Jim used coal dust to make the word 'Cloud' on the snow, and it guided in a helicopter carrying insulin.

In 1922 Sir Edward Mountain, urgently recalled to London, had a team of fourteen men dig a seven-mile path through deep snow so that he could ride his horse to Porlock. He lived at grim-faced Oare Manor, hard by the church, in succession to a long line of Snows, who first acquired the property in the early 18th century. The last of the line, the renowned Nicholas Snow, is described in his memorial tablet as:

Lord of the Manor of Oare
an Upright Man greatly skilled in woodcraft
Master of Hounds.

Since Nicholas had taken offence at the portrayal of a Snowe (sic) in *Lorna Doone,* R. D. Blackmore presented him—by way of a peace offering—with a silver two-handled cup inscribed:

R. D. Blackmore
1875
Nicholas Snow
Oare Farm
1877

In fact, as F. J. Snell pointed out in his *The Blackmore Country* the Snows did not become landowners at Oare until long after the period of the Doone story. Nicholas must, however, have buried the hatchet because, when the Prince of Wales—later Edward VII—came for a day's hunting in August 1879, he took tea at Oare Manor and drank ale from the Blackmore Cup. That day went down in local history and is described in detail in Marshall's book. The Prince came to Exmoor at the invitation of Parson Jack Russell of Swimbridge and Landkey, renowned equally as a good country priest, hunting man, and breeder of the terriers that bear his name. On that August day the entire countryside turned out. Arthur Heal, the huntsman, brought the hounds over from Exford to Hawkcombe Head where, shortly before noon, the Prince arrived with his host, Claud Luttrell of Dunster Castle. The party then moved on to Culbone Stables, where the Prince—sitting on his horse, eating bread and cheese—was respectfully addressed by the farmers as 'Mister Purnce'. At the end of the day, after a good run, the stag—brought to bay close to the 'Doone Houses' by Badgworthy Water—was given the *coup de grace* by the Prince himself, using Arthur Heal's hunting knife.

Doone legends abounded here when the schoolboy Blackmore visited his grandfather's parsonage that is now the long slate-roofed house of Parsonage Farm, and returned years later to revive his memories. At the Parsonage he picked up 'Prick the calf and the cow'll moo', horrible saying of a Doone who, intent on murder and loot, tormented a child while a servant girl cowered among the faggots. A mile from the church Blackmore stood on Robber's Bridge at Oareford where the Doones divided their spoil.

The hymn, *As pants the hart for cooling streams,* has been sung many a time in Oare Church, as at Exford, just before the opening of the hunt season and at funerals of huntsmen. At the funeral of one old stag harbourer, the congregation had come out into the churchyard and were astounded to see 'six great stags above Deddycombe, motionless, gazing down'. In tears an old man cried out, 'Twas bound to happen'.

PARRACOMBE   O.S. 670450

St. Petrock, so they say, built his tiny wattle church on the height east of the combe in which the village lies, and marked on the map as 'Churchtown'. Tracy, one of the murderers of Thomas à Becket, expressed remorse by giving the 12th century building its tower—

again, so they say. In the 18th century it acquired furnishings and a simplicity of interior that has made it the perfect example of a remote village church of that period. So strong is its unadorned rustic charm that its hundreds of visitors can almost conjure up the band of musicians on the sloped seats at the west end, the congregation in their box pews, the parson in the three-decker pulpit. Young Bradley, who walked over from Challacombe some Sunday afternoons mainly to pick up *The Field* at the post office, long remembered the stark whiteness of the walls, the fiddlers accompanying the hymns, the clerk droning the metrical psalms in broad Devon dialect. In 1878-9 when the old church was threatened with destruction, John Ruskin raised his voice to great effect and contributed towards the building of a new and separate Victorian Gothic parish church, raised on the northern slope of the village. St. Petrock's was saved; and it was saved again by common effort in 1970, by which time the fabric had dangerously decayed. The restoration was celebrated on Trinity Sunday 1972 when a crowded congregation saw a 10-year-old Revel Queen enter the church behind the clergy and heard music from a string quartet in the old musicians' seats. St. Petrock's remains in good order and occasional use. Beside it stands the long, slated, church house, now converted into two cottages, where villagers used to brew and drink ale and disport themselves on feast days on the grassy green outside.

This is a true moorland village, surrounded by superb Exmoor landscape: moors holding woods in their clefts, milk-white streams, fields full of sheep and often black with rooks. Its ancient origin is emphasised by the remarkably well preserved remains of Holwell Castle, named supposedly after some lost holy well. In *Exmoor Review 1982* Charles Whybrow, the antiquarian, wrote:

Holwell Castle is almost a textbook model of the earthwork of a Norman private fortress. Every detail of the motte, bailey ramparts, gateway and moats can still be clearly seen . . . its position, overlooking the older part of the village and the ancient ford (where now stands the bridge), is within a few hundred yards of important medieval cross-roads.

The village has a dignified comeliness, born of the narrow streets and of the pink, cream, white and grey houses built of local stone with slate roofs. There are complaints of water shortage, yet the lanes are often streaming wet and encourage huge ferns to flourish under the beech hedges. At the bottom of the combe the infant Heddon rushes between stone walls. Impetuous in its haste to reach Heddon's Mouth, it found its way into Lionel Johnson's *Lynton Verses:*

It took three lives in the Lynmouth flood disaster of 1952. The Fox and Goose Inn receives travellers warmly, even though the hostelry rules of 1786 face them over the bar:

> No Thieves, Fakirs, Rogues or Tinkers
> No Slap and Tickle of the Wenches
> No Banging of Tankards on Tables.

A picture shows an earlier thatched building. Parracombe had its brewery also, sited in the small car park over the bridge. The landlord possesses one of its green glass bottles lettered 'Crocombe & Son, Parracombe'. The former Malthouse, opposite the car park, is a lovingly tended flag-stoned cottage behind which, in 1962, Peter Teal and his wife found the old mill, twenty years disused. In the *Exmoor Review 1968* is a description of how they restored the leat and the wheel, and adapted it to generate electricity to dry the timber he used to make spinning wheels, and turn the lathes upon which they were made.

In 1926 the lively artist Walter Wilkinson brought his puppet theatre on a tour of Exmoor villages and, as he recounts in his book, *The Peep Show,* found Parracombe an endearing place. Here he camped untroubled in a buttercup field among geese and set up his show on the cobbled space near the inn.

When the little Lynton—Barnstaple line was opened in 1898, Parracombe was provided with a halt and a supply of water for the locomotives. Tickets were sold at the post office. Passengers however were rarely numerous and it fell to the guard to deal with any business when the train stopped at the halt. A pleasant note was struck by the rector and local historian, the Rev. J. F. Chanter, whose custom it was to scatter flower seeds from the carriage window.

PORLOCK   *O.S. 885468*

Centuries ago Porlock had a harbour of its own, at the place the Saxons called 'the enclosure by the harbour'. It was there that Danish invaders beached their boats in AD 918, and that—not long before the Norman Conquest—Saxon Harold landed to loot the neighbourhood.

To east and west Porlock is enclosed by towering hills. On the seaward side it is bounded by the Marsh, confined by a broad crescent of grey shingle. Beyond this barrier a low tide will sometimes reveal stumps of trees — relics of the so-called 'submarine forest'—submerged by the rise in sea level several thousand years ago. The town itself sits in Porlock Vale that stretches inland to form the most fertile area of farm land in the National Park, growing some of the best barley in the country. It is all bird territory too. Seabirds and songbirds frequent the Marsh in huge numbers. In winter, curlew and lapwing cry through the mist, and angular herons stand by the pools. The Vale is a great migration path along which stream swallows, wheatears, warblers, sandpipers, wagtails; many linger through spring and summer. E. W. Hendy recorded their life pattern in detail, as has N. V. Allen in his *The Birds of Exmoor,* and in other publications of the Exmoor Natural History Society.

Porlock's sheltered position gives it a mild climate that creates a paradise of flowers. 'Thatch . ..dark interiors within open doors . . . yellow roses on cottage walls, charmingly mated with stucco', wrote Henry James. Today walls are festooned with roses, wistaria, jasmine and honeysuckle; while, in the gardens, myrtles, fuchsias, hollyhocks, camellias, azaleas and hydrangeas provide a feast of colour. What is left of the traditional architecture is picturesque and characteristic of an old sea settlement —thatched cottages with backs to the street, external bread ovens, and tall rounded chimneys on sturdy square bases. It was all like this, no doubt, but dirtier, when Collinson wrote his history of Somerset in 1791:

Most of the houses form two mean straggling streets near the church and are chiefly built of rough stone or mud walls, and the fields are so deep that no carriages of any kind can be used.

Seven years later, when sitting in the corner of the parlour of the Ship Inn and writing a mediocre sonnet for the *Morning Post,* Robert Southey was kinder. In his journal he noted:

This place is called in the neighbourhood 'The End of the World'. All beyond is inaccessible to carriage or even cart. A sort of sledge is used by the country people, resting upon two poles like cart shafts.

Southey praised the well-furnished pretty old inn and enjoyed the potted seaweed-delicacy laverbread with his breakfast, loving it ever after. Coleridge, his brother-in-law, must also have known The Ship. So did Blackmore's Tom Faggus and John Ridd, who bought powder for his blunderbuss at 'The Spit and Gridiron' shop, afterwards riding up daunting Porlock Hill, using the route his father followed from Porlock market, before his murder by the Doones on the high moor.

In a highly informative article in the *Exmoor Review 1973*, W. R. Hedley explained the reasons for Porlock's poverty in Southey's day. The home industries of spinning and weaving were losing out to the new textile factories in the north. Exports had been hit by the Napoleonic wars; and about this time the herring trade failed, due to the movement of the fish away from the Bristol Channel. Hadley added:

It was Porlock's misfortune that during the 18th century there was no resident rector or squire. The manor of Porlock passed into the Blathwayt family in 1707, but they preferred to live in their fine house at Dyrham Park, near Bath. On the church side, the Rev. Clarke, when he became Rector in 1831, was the first resident rector for over 100 years.

However, the population rose steadily all during the 19th century. The first stage coach arrived in 1843, and this became a feature of Porlock life until the service stopped in the early 1920s. Porlock Hill was first climbed by a motor car in 1901, and in 1916 the first motor bus appeared. By the turn of the century the tourist trade was growing apace, with several hotels, apartments to let, a variety of shops and trades (including notably riding stables, saddlers and blacksmiths, some still in evidence today), and a

Porlock—roofs and truncated spire.

H. H. Hole

77

number of social changes, many of them initiated by the Rev. Walter Hook, incumbent of the parish church of St. Dubricius. With its truncated spire (the top was lost during a storm in 1700), this is a striking and historic building. The spire, incidentally, was re-clothed with oak shingles by that fine craftsman, Philip Burgess, leatherworker of West Porlock.

The old priest's house called Chantry Cottage stands near the churchyard, where tombstones are inscribed with quaint epitaphs, long-standing names like Moule, Huish, Ridler, and charming old-fashioned girls' names such as Phoebe, Salome, Joanna, and Ilett. The unique clock in the tower, no hands, no face, struck the hours on the tenor bell for nearly 500 years after Roger Clockmaker of Barnstaple made it in c.1400. The church has beautiful lancet windows, a parvise chamber, a 13th century arcade, and a modern reredos of gilded wood painted with figures of Celtic missionary saints, including Porlock's own St. Dubricius who, as Tennyson reminds us, solemnised Arthur's marriage to Guinevere. In a wall recess lies the yellow stone effigy of a crusader. Among other objects of beauty and interest are the canopied effigies of Sir John Harington wearing a rose-garlanded helmet—he fought at Agincourt—and his wife, Elizabeth, who wears a demure padded lacy headdress. 'Lingered in the cool timber-steepled church, betwixt manorial pew and battered tomb of crusading knight and lady', wrote Henry James. A brass tablet commemorates the Phelps family. Richard, who died in 1785, no great artist, was a fashionable portraitist in his day. He painted members of several leading Somerset families: Palmer, Popham, and Luttrell among them.

Porlock Weir

V.B.C.

PORLOCK WEIR   O.S. 865478

The present harbour was formed out of a natural creek and a
quay built in the last century, with a wall and lock gates to the east.
For long the place was busy with the import of culm and limestone,
and the export of farm produce, bark for tanning, and livestock. As
Grahame Farr has recorded in his book, *Ships and Harbours of
Exmoor:*

> In 1858 William Pulsford built his own smack, the *John and William,* at the back of the
> harbour, and as far as we can trace she was the only trader ever built there . . . Several other
> small craft were owned at Porlock . . . The largest of the Porlock craft was Edward Perkins'
> schooner, *Flying Foam,* 85 tons . . . Last of the locally owned traders was the ketch *Mistletoe,*
> built at Plymouth in 1890 for Thomas Ley of Combe Martin . . . About 1950 the last sea-
> borne coal cargo came in the ubiquitous *Democrat.*

Nowadays the harbour is full of yachts in the summer, and there
is plenty of patronage for the two hotels and handful of shops.

'Porlock Weir goes nowhere else' wrote the artist Cecil Aldin in
1935, much as Southey had described Porlock itself in 1798. Indeed
it is a physical dead end. To go somewhere else you must take the
road past the old manor house of Worthy. Hollies, larches, birches
and bracken make a screen of variegated green on your left, ferns
trail in the cascading stream, the crinkled sea glitters far below on
your right. From Ashley Combe Lodge the toll road climbs and
turns through the 'hanging woods', as Dorothy Wordsworth (who
had no toll road) called them, until it runs out at Hawkcombe Head
on the way to Lynton. The alternative way is along the serpentine
cliffside path to Culbone, which Coleridge took in 1797 on his way
up to Ash Farm. He came to the house of rough grey-red masonry
yellowed by lichen, protected on its seaward side by its barns. From
a stile he could survey a pattern of steeply falling fields, woods,
rocks, the sea, a purple headland. All these, bathed in moonlight, he
put into his poetic drama, *Osorio,* written soon afterwards.

By a fireside at the farm he sat reading a travel book, *Purchas's
Pilgrimage,* after taking two grains of opium—freely available to
anyone — for an internal ailment, and fell asleep to dream a fantasy
that his brain wove into a poem filled with gorgeous imagery. He
awoke and had set down some fifty lines with ease when 'a person
from Porlock' arrived to visit him. Who? What for? All we know is
that the person checked the composition of *Kubla Khan* 'An oaf
from Porlock knocked and blundered', wrote Siegried Sasson in
some satiric verse, when staying in the village. It is just possible that

Coleridge stayed, not at Ash, but at Broomstreet Farm, as years later when trying to recall the name, he said it resembled the word 'brimstone'.

In 1800 the Rev. Richard Warner rode up the road to Lord King's cottage, Ashley Lodge, 'which creeps through woods which clothe steep cliffs'. He called the house 'a singular mansion, placed like an eagle's nest in a cleft of rock . . . a small castellated dwelling, . . . the view is the *only* charm'. Nevertheless the next Lord King, who became the Earl of Lovelace, brought his wife Ada, daughter of Lord Byron, to live here in the summer. About 1865 they built a larger mansion called Ashley Combe, an Italianate house with a campanile. Dr. Barnardo's boys lived there during the second world war. The house has since been demolished, and some of its stones are built into a garden wall just outside Porlock. Lord Lytton, the last owner, incorporated features of Ashley Combe (e.g. the Magnolia Room) in his novel, *Mickla Bendore*.

ROADWATER   *O.S. 035385*

At the bottom of the Roadwater valley and just outside the National Park lie the remains of Cleeve Abbey, a farming community of monks and the only Cistercian house in Somerset, founded in 1189 and dissolved by Henry VIII in 1537. Built of a faded-rose sandstone and wearing the patina of age, Cleeve is far from being a forlorn remnant, as the gatehouse and domestic buildings, admirably restored and cared for by the Department of the Environment, remain almost intact. The rapid Roadwater stream worked the abbey mill. The Cistercians called this valley 'Vallis Florida', or Flowery Valley. Flowery it is: wild flowers of stream and hedgebank grow on the field side, while the gardens of houses and cottages are bright with the colours of wallflowers, saxifrage, roses, peonies, fuchsias, dahlias, according to the season. The stream rushes and tumbles down the whole length of the valley and breaks into a noisy waterfall. Close to the water stands a pretty cottage of historical interest, as it occupies the site of a wayside chapel dedicated to St. Pancras. Little remains of the chapel except one small lancet window, but in the garden there is the holy well of St. Pancras of clear and unfailing water, with old stone-work partly overgrown by moss and ferns.

Down the valley used to run the 'old mineral line', officially the West Somerset Mineral Railway, built from the port of Watchet via Roadwater to Comberow in 1857, and thereafter up the massive incline (three quarters of a mile long at a gradient of 1 in 4) to the top of Brendon Hill, for the transport of iron ore from the mines in the neighbourhood of Raleghs Cross. While mining ceased in 1883, the passenger service to Comberow survived untill 1898. A limited revival took place 1907-10, but all rails and rolling stock were removed at the end of the first world war. The old Roadwater station is now a house; another dwelling has been made out of a former railway wagon.

Not far away in a garden, there is a weather-faded board bearing the dragon emblem of the Somerset Guild of Craftsmen. Here until a few years ago were the premises of Harry Horrobin, notable craftsman who, with his son, James, designed and fashioned fine examples of wrought-iron gates, brackets, lanterns, door-knockers, and much else—that won national prizes and are now to be seen in Exmoor villages such as Winsford and Dulverton, and in places outside the National Park altogether. While James carries on the business at Carhampton, Harry has now turned his skill to making violins and cellos. Another artist, Rachel Reckitt of Golsoncott, made the arresting painted metalwork wign for The Valiant Soldier inn, also the sign for The White Horse further down the valley; and it was her family that gave Roadwater its village hall fifty years ago.

In his book, *The Old Mineral Line,* also in *Exmoor Review 1977,* R. J. Sellick has given an account of Daniel Nethercott, born in 1829, a stone mason who also became an early photographer without abandoning his original craft. Nethercott set up a dark room at his relatives' farmhouse in Druid's Combe—the older name is Drucombe—a beautiful spot reached by following the stream's course upward through the valley, where the water flows over smooth red-brown stones, and where cones strew the ground from many rustling larches and firs.

A number of Nethercott's photographs are preserved by Dr Glyn Court, who has reproduced several in his *West Somerset in Times Past,* and whose uncle, The Rev. Lewis Court, told the story of local Methodism—always strong in this area—in *The Romance of a Country Circuit.* Dr Court, himself an organist at Roadwater chapel, has published a collection of charming old Brendon Hill carols and an account of the remarkable Thomas Slade, blacksmith, who saved to buy a cello (bass viol), played it well, and conducted a band of Roadwater musicians. It was their practice to sing and play carols outside houses and on the bridge every Christmas Eve. At the Revels, Slade replaced the equally remarkable George Matthews of Leighland—the musicians still playing, after Matthews' death, the Roadwater Quick Step and other pieces he had composed for their village.

The Gatehouse, Cleeve Abbey

Colin Thornton

RODHUISH

This is a peaceful pretty place, wrapped in a patchwork of green-and-gold fields in summertime, with roses tumbling over stone garden walls and valerian blooming of sandstone barns. To the west rise the steep and wooded slopes of Croydon Hill, Monkham Hill and Slowley Wood. Approached by ancient lanes, worn deep by centuries of weather and generations of pedestrians and horsemen, difficulty of access has caused some chroniclers to overlook Rodhuish altogether. In 1791 Collinson dismissed it as 'twenty houses and a small chapel'. This was 'the ancient chapelry of St. Bartholomew', to which, in Catholic times, parishioners and their priest processed at Rogation-tide and other festivals, sometimes following the course of the Pill River. They stopped at certain houses and farms, 'the widow Doddridge's' and 'George Escott's house', the priest 'saying a gospell' at each as well as receiving refreshment. By the 18th century the Escotts had become prominent as landowners and benefactors of the parish. Richard Escott gave the church a chalice, napkin, and silver plate, paid the priest when he administered the sacrament to aged poor people unable to struggle up to St. Bartholomew's, and gave money to provide a school for 20 children and pay a 'dame' as teacher. The family name is perpetuated in Escott Farm and Escott Wood, where a stream used to turn Escott Mill.

A more sinister and disorderly procession occasionally straggled through lanes leading to the oak tree called Felon's Oak in a lane that in April becomes a Paradise of primroses. Tradition insists that the oak made a gallows—probably for sheep stealers, caught in the act and summarily hanged, some being buried on the spot. Close by are the gates of Croydon Hall, now a special school for maladjusted children of junior age, but formerly the property of Count Conrad von Hochberg, an Anglophile German aristocrat, who disappeared suddenly and mysteriously just before the first world war—see Jack Hurley's *Murder and Mystery on Exmoor*. At Lodge House lived Hubert Herkomer, etcher and painter, professor and member of the Royal Academy. He was a friend of the artist, John William North, and illustrated Thomas Hardy's *Tess of the D'Urbervilles*.

In the late 1700s the little church 'on its lonely knoll' was served several times by the Rev. James Newton, learned friend of Samuel Taylor Coleridge. Early in this century it was in the care of the Rev.

Alec Locke, who was presented in 1917 to the living of Carhampton-cum-Rodhuish. In *Exmoor Review 1981* his daughter, Anne, described how, as a small girl, she would sometimes accompany him on her pony, when he rode back and forth between his churches on a chestnut cob. When older she would drive him in a pony cart, and on special Sundays—when Rodhuish had two services—they both enjoyed a splendid dinner at one of the hospitable farmhouses. About this time the lanes were trudged by zealous and devoted local preachers, who ministered to the little iron chapel built by Bible Christians in 1899 and known as the 'tin tabernacle'.

The ancient 'chapelry' still makes the hamlet's heart; recently the sum of £165 was raised in one afternoon at Oak in a corner of the parish to pay for repairs and decoration. It still receives gifts, such as flowering trees for the churchyard, and latterly embroideries from Beatrice Reckitt, mother of the artist, Rachel Reckitt, whose own work graces several Exmoor churches.

SIMONSBATH   O.S. 773393

The meaning of the name has never been elucidated, though undoubtedly of ancient origin, but it must have had some significance as being in the heart of the old Royal Forest, which remained Crown property until its enclosure in 1815—the principal portion then being sold to John Knight, the Midland ironmaster, in 1818. For centuries before this it had been leased to wardens, who had made what they could out of renting summer grazing to local farmers, and who had maintained its boundaries, and otherwise kept it in good order, with the help of the Free Suitors and certain others who held customary rights. The history is a complex one, superbly set out in *The History of Exmoor Forest* by E. T. MacDermot, and summarised in S. H. Burton's book, *Exmoor*.

Simonsbath Lodge, the handsome E-shaped building we see to-day, was the first house proper in the Forest, and completed in 1654 by James Boevey, an eccentric, quarrelsome London merchant of Flemish descent, who had bought the freehold of the Forest from Parliament in 1651, and who surprisingly retained possession on lease after the Restoration of the monarchy in 1660. But it was the vast enterprise of John Knight and his son, Frederic, conducted between c.1820 and c.1890, that caught public interest and was responsible for the appearance of much of Exmoor today. Roads built; thousands of acres of moorland reclaimed and cultivated; some fifteen farms founded with names such as Honeymead, Warren, Horsen, Wintershead, Larkbarrow, etc.; large-scale experiments in crop and livestock husbandry; mining; the building of miles of banks topped by beech hedges; the planting of windbreaks; the creation of Simonsbath village and the parish of Exmoor. All this is recorded in C. S. Orwin's classic *The Reclamation of Exmoor Forest,* and best read in the edition, revised and updated by R. J. Sellick.

Most of the anecdotes and incidents of human and literary interest relate to the last 150 years. In his rambling but lively *Reminiscences,* the Rev. W. H. Thornton, formerly curate at Countisbury and first incumbent of the parish of Exmoor (1856-61), left some fascinating notes and observations. At Simonsbath, for example, he found that the builder (or possibly the clerk of works) was acting dishonestly— installing 'light' lead and poor piping at the rectory, and using Bath stone of an inferior quality for the church, so that it peeled off in flakes at the first severe frost. Thornton went everywhere on his horse, thinking nothing of riding 25 miles to visit a couple of parishioners; holding two services on Sunday at Simonsbath and a third at Sandyway; helping out at the school. In 1858 he left Exeter one day at 3 p.m. and dined at home 42 miles away at 8 p.m. In the course of five years he married, raised a family, and played the part of spiritual factotum to his 500 or so parishioners. On one unforgettable occasion in 1858 he acted the part of Sherlock Holmes. William Burgess, a local bad character who lodged at Gallon House, was suspected of murdering his little daughter, Anna Maria. Both of them had disappeared. Burgess was picked up at Swansea, but there was no sign of the child. Thornton then confronted him and publicly accused him of murder, but without any corroborative evidence. Three months went by and then, thanks to 'information received', the investigators were directed to the Wheal Eliza mine on the River Barle below Simonsbath. A volunteer was lowered into the shaft and, eventually, was hauled up again carrying a seaman's tarpaulin coat tied around with cord. Thornton cut the cord, slit open a guano bag inside, and found the remains of poor little Anna Maria. Burgess confessed, was taken to Taunton, and hanged.

In his *Exploration of Exmoor,* J.Ll.W. Page wrote that, thirty years later, 'without knowing aught of the tragedy', he experienced:

a distinct feeling of depression as I climbed the track behind the haunted ruin, through the rain if an autumn evening.

Another eerie place was the one where John Knight had dammed the waters of the infant Barle to make the lake called Pinkery Pond. Henry Williamson sensed its sinister emanations in his book, *Devon Holiday.*

The water at the shallow edges is clear but yellow-brown from the peat; at the lower end it is cold, black, deep . . . the rushy verge trodden by wild ponies and deer . . . monsters are lurking down there.

In 1889, after a lovelorn farmer's suicide, men tried to locate his body by floating a loaf bearing a lighted candle on the water — without success. Then they partially drained the pond by withdrawing one of the two great plugs in the double drain pipes — and found what they were looking for.

But it would be wrong to paint this part of Exmoor solely in sombre colours. Sir John Fortescue, historian of the British Army, came here to fish, ride and hunt. In his *Records of Staghunting on Exmoor,* he mentioned seeing rare birds such as the snowy owl, Montagu's harrier, ravens; and wild animals like badger and

Simonsbath Lodge

Rev. W. A. Bevis

polecat. In 1897 he wrote the children's classic tale, *Story of a Red Deer*, 'as the deer have told it to me in many a long ride'. It contains felicitous descriptions of Horner oakwoods carpeted in primroses, of Dunkery marked by brown turf-pits and great stones, of peaty streams 'like brown ale'. And all of a deer's life from its birth in the fern. The cairn raised to Sir John's memory is set high up beside the road to Kinsford Gate.

'Beloved old Simonsbath, I should like to have seen it again', said W. H. Hudson, a day or two before his death. 'He remembered its wildness and its birds', wrote his biographer.

SELWORTHY and *HOLNICOTE*

O.S. 920468

O.S. 911463

As elsewhere on Exmoor both Selworthy and Holnicote have ancient origins and associations. For example, an Iron Age fort called Bury Castle, stands at a short distance to the north-west of Selworthy church, and according to J. K. Ridler, writing in *A Selworthy Notebook,* there is evidence in field names of Danish incursions inland when they raided Porlock in the 10th century AD. Manorial and medieval history is recorded in detail by Charles E. H. Chadwyck Healey in his *History of Part of West Somerset.* But for most people the two places are indissolubly linked with the Acland family who first established themselves here in the middle of the 18th century.

Through his marriage in 1745 to Elizabeth Dyke, Sir Thomas Acland (7th baronet)—first of a long line of Thomases — already in possession of properties at Killerton, near Exeter, and Petherton, near Bridgwater, found himself—in the words of Anne Acland, historian of the family:

. . . master of three separate new estates in Somerset, based on three family houses at Holnicote, near Porlock, Pixton, near Dulverton, and Tetton, near Taunton.

Sir Thomas was typical of his class and age. A keen racing man, he was also Master of the North Devon Staghounds for thirty years and, by leasing the wardenship of the Royal Forest of Exmoor in 1767, able to give full rein to his sporting interests. From 1746 he represented Devon in Parliament with Sir William Courtenay. To quote Anne Acland again (p.16 of her book, *A Devon Family*):

Selworthy Green

V.B.C.

Many squires could remember, as Sir Thomas could, that their grandfathers or great-grandfathers had fought in the Civil War, and feel thankful that peaceful times now made it possible for them to husband their estates, re-build and furnish their houses when they wished to, and, above all, to enjoy their possessions to the fullest possible extent. It was no shame to drink, gamble, cockfight, or beget children out of wedlock. The 7th baronet did all these things, and yet died as well respected as any man in the West of England.

Now followed a series of mishaps, if not disasters. Holnicote was burned down, for the first time, in 1779. Sir Thomas died in 1785. His elder son, John, died after being captured in the American War of Independence. His grandson, also John (8th baronet), died at the age of seven. His younger son, Thomas (9th baronet), a promising young man, died in 1794. Then however began the reign of the two great Sir Thomases, one after the other, which virtually spanned the rest of the century. The 10th baronet (1787-1871), known familiarly as 'Ole Zur Tummus', was the last to wear the famous beaver-skin hat, and sat in Parliament for 45 years, having spent—it was estimated—not less than £80,000 on his elections! He it was who planted some 800,000 trees between 1810 and 1826 (now in the care of the National Trust) that we see and enjoy today, and otherwise devoted a great deal of time and resources to the improvement of his estates. At the age of 21, he married Lydia, daughter of the banker,

Henry Hoare who—on hearing on one occasion that the young couple were temporarily short of money and would have to live by their wits, remarked that

. . . he was very sorry to hear it, for two people more unfitted to live by their wits than his daughter, Lydia, and her husband, Tom Acland, he had never known.

Being a great landowner and Member of Parliament was a restless life, and involved commuting between the various family houses, each one fully furnished and equipped with complete sets of linen, glass and silver, ready for occupation at a moment's notice. Holnicote served more or less as a holiday home, and had to be rebuilt after it was burned down for the second time in 1851. This pattern of life was also followed by the 11th baronet, the last of the Sir Thomases, a generous and caring landlord in the period of agricultural depresion, and friend of Gladstone whom he only survived by ten days at death in 1898.

The other centre of life at Selworthy was the church and its incumbent: notably the Rev. Joshua Stevenson, rector 1802-63, close friend of the Aclands, and who became 'as much a family chaplain as a parish priest'. In his old age he was assisted by the Rev. Archer Thompson, whose daughter, Marianne, recalled in later years:

As a child I thought looking towards Dunkery from the Cross [in the churchyard] was like a peep into Heaven. I think growing up in such a country was a great blessing to me. I learnt at Selworthy to care for all things beautiful.

On a March day when a robin flutes in one of the glittering hollies and when snowdrops sprinkle the Green, Selworthy still resembles a picture in a child's old-fashioned story book; yet it is hardly a genuine village, lacking children school, inn, and ordinary shops. The Green was created as a tiny commune in 1810 by Sir Thomas the 10th, who used part of an old farmhouse and dilapidated farm buildings to construct white cottages with rounded chimneys, external bread ovens and latticed windows, for his servants to occupy. Little Marianne delighted in these fairytale dwellings what her mother sketched, in visiting the old lady with the last spinning-wheel in Selworthy, and the basketmaker seated under the walnut tree. Together they sought out rare ferns, penetrated the woods to see the little spring called katherine's Well and, higher up, Agnes's Fountain, welling out of a fissure between small rocks that in winter the frost transformed into a jewelled grotto.

The gabled buttressed 15th century Tithe Barn stands opposite the Green. A carved pig, lamb and wheatsheaf are still just discernible on the hood mould of a blocked window. The Barn has now become a house where, some time after the second world war, Walter and Winifred Wilkinson came to live—an extraordinary, witty and lovable couple. In her seventies Winifred wrote several novels of considerable power and perception. Gollancz, the publisher, wrote that he had never been more struck by an MS than by her *God in Hell,* based on her experiences as a relief worker in Poland. In their younger days the Wilkinsons had toured the countryside with their puppet shows, including a number of Exmoor villages.

Sited with a magnificent view of Dunkery, Robin How, and the wooded slopes of Horner and Luccombe, the church itself is an architectural treasure, its interior so full of interest that only a visit can do it justice. As Page pointed out, despite damage in the Civil War, the handsomest part is the south aisle built in 1538 and lighted by Perpendicular Gothic windows of large size and well-cut tracery. It has a roof adorned with carved and gilded bosses depicting angels, saints, emblems of the Passion, a variety of flowers and symbols. The east window of the north aisle contains pieces of medieval glass glowing with rich red and azure. The reredos of embossed leatherwork was created by Philip Burgess of Porlock. The carved oak pulpit has a good sounding board and hour glass. The west gallery, now housing the organ, was where Marianne Thompson saw Joseph Stenner, carpenter, drag his cello to play with the other musicians at Sunday services; and the high balcony pew, whence the squire surveyed the congregation.

During a lull in his mortal illness in 1887, Richard Jefferies wrote with unimpaired clarity of Selworthy Woods breathless in heat, of the declining sun filling dark combes at the side of Dunkery with light, of humble bees in holly flowers, and of squirrels playing on the lawns of Holnicote House.

STOKE PERO   *O.S. 878435*

Before the present century, time had wrought little change in this small place. Even now its ancient pattern survives almost intact. A handful of settlers planted it over 1,000 feet up—they may have been Celts preceding the Saxons who gave it the humdrum name of

Stoke, meaning 'enclosure' or 'settlement'. Pero is derived from Pyrow or Piro, the family to whom the land was granted after the Norman Conquest. Almost all the nine or ten farms found in Stoke Pero today were occupied at the time that Domesday Book was made, and several have names as ancient, e.g. Lucott. The country is full of contrasts — steep valleys and dense woodlands, with Dunkery rising above them, brooding over the little church set in a grassy hollow or bowl so deep that its present dumpy tower just overtops the brim.

Incumbents came and went, probably because of its 'littleness and loneliness'.

Culbone, Oare and Stoke Pero
Parishes three no parson'll go to.

In the *Exmoor Review 1968,* Arthur Elliott-Cannon recorded that during the Black Death the parish had no fewer than three priests inside twelve months, and that in 1369, Robert Thoryng distinguished himself by abducting the wife of one of his parishioners, 'Alice from Bucketthole'. Parsons lived intermittently at this lonely place, in a parsonage near the church; but long gaps in the records suggest that—during the 18th century at least—no permanent appointment was made and that, if services were held at all, they were the responsibility—as they are today—of the Porlock rector. Church life revived when Parson Gould came in 1857, and in 1897 the whole building was restored by Sir Thomas Acland (11th baronet). As Elliott-Cannon pointed out:

We see not simply a restoration, but a new church on an ancient site. Some mediaeval window frames have been incorporated, and old stones re-used; but there is little to remind us of the ancient building except a mediaeval door with door-posts cut from two enormous blocks of oak, and a font of indeterminate age . . . The roof is rather splendid, with barrel-shaped oak beams, every fourth beam bearing a carved coat of arms or motif. All this timber was borne here by a Porlock donkey named Zulu, who padded his way twice a day from Parson Street, Porlock, to Stoke Pero, for many months in 1897. It seems fitting in this simple church that Zulu should be commemorated, even if only with a framed notice.

The poverty of the place was attested on several occasions at different stages of history. In 1796 the parish cultivated only four acres of wheat. Locke, who reached it with great difficulty a few years later found 'fourteen mean-looking dwellings'. He hoped for a drink of ale at the public house kept by the parish clerk, but was disappointed to learn that the Sir Thomas Acland of the day had revoked its licence, because the previous landlady had buried two husbands 'near the cellar door'— actually in the adjoining churchyard! The house is now Church Farm, standing with its red sandstone buildings beside the church in the hollow. Some years later in his *History of the Hundred of Carhampton,* James Savage noted:

There is much woodland and some healthy wilds; the roads are few and bad, and not much used; they are impassable for any carriages, being so steep, narrow, and incumbered with large loose stones, that they are, generally speaking, dangerous even for horses; in short, the inhabitants have very little intercourse with the rest of the world, the parish being as isolated a spot as any in the whole country.

Nevertheless he was struck by the 'wild romantick' aspect of the place, the hillsides covered by mosses and whortleberry, the wooded combes with the rushing Horner and its attendant rivulets full of trout, running through them. He learned that an old woman, receiving 'parish pay' taught a few children to read, and that eloping couples came to this secret place to get married.

Some apocryphal stories are told about Stoke Pero. Of Parson Gould being involved in an altercation with Farmer Heywood one Sunday morning over the day of the month for the psalm, and of the latter settling the matter by reference to Old Moore's Almanack over a glass of cider in the farmhouse where the service was concluded. And of a missionary sermon that went, according to Marshall, as follows:

'I've been axed', said the old rector, 'to have a collection in this church for the S.P.G. I don't know exactly what the S.P.G. is for, but I fancy 'tis something to do with providing petticoats for the niggers in Africa. If anybody likes to put tuppence or drappence in the plate he can if he be minded to, but I b'ant going to'.

TARR STEPS   *O.S. 868322*

The origins of this well-known clapper bridge across the river Barle, midway between Withypool and Dulverton, and of its name, have never been settled. As regards the name, L. V. Grinsell in his book, *The Archaeology of Exmoor,* dismissed the variant *torr,* which usually means 'a place on high ground', obviously not applicable here. Another possibility is *tochar,* a Celtic word meaning 'causeway', which seems plausible but is not supported by Celtic scholars. In *Exmoor Review 1972,* Hazel Eardley-Wilmot suggested the Sanskrit word *tara,* meaning in essence a 'crossing'; and if that is as likely a solution as any, then it could take us back to the Bronze Age people, deep in the mists of time, who left no inscription or written record of any kind—probably they could not write—but

Tarr Steps

Colin Thornton

they must have crossed the Barle where the Steps stand, if only at the ford when the river was low. As to the bridge itself—180 feet long, 17 spans, the cover-slabs 4-5 feet wide, standing on massive stone piers laid on the river bed—it is now considered to be of medieval construction. Although badly damaged in the 1952 flood, and shifted more than once since, it has always been carefully re-instated and stands today as strong as ever, arousing admiration and wonder.

The sight of those 'stone planks' as Richard Jeffries called them, laid upon the stone buttresses across the Barle who 'comes with his natural rush and fierceness under the stone planking', has drawn innumerable artists, travellers and photographers. 'There can be no doubt of the loveliness of the spot', Jefferies continued, and his keen eye observed 'broad golden cups' of marsh marigolds overhanging a pool, brown trout darting from under the slabs, the horned sheep crossing the bridge.

Tennyson came here in 1891. 'We drove through the Barle Valley to Hawkridge, then to Tarr Steps', wrote his son. 'Some tawny cows were cooling themselves in mid-stream, green meadows on one side, on the other a wooded slope'.

93

The green meadows and tawny cows belonged to remote Ashway Farm on the eastern side of the river, 'the last farmstead before the pathless moor', wrote the biographer of Sir George Williams. The boy George Williams born here, spent his early years helping his father—a tenant farmer described as a yeoman—with his sheep and cattle, sometimes driving them down to the path to Tarr Steps. George attended Mrs Timlett's school in Dulverton High Street, and in the course of time became the renowned founder of the Young Men's Christian Association, some years after his apprenticeship to a drapery store in Bridgwater. His father died of a bite from a moorland adder.

Old Ashway, on the further side of the Varle Hill, was the base for the Acland herd of Exmoor ponies that ran out on Winsford Hill. In *Exmoor Review 1970,* F. H. Reeks—agent to the Acland estate that passed to the National Trust in 1944—gave an interesting account of the autumn round-ups, followed by inspections for entry in the Stud Book. The ponies were often young and wild, and handling them was an exciting experience.

TIMBERSCOMBE   *O.P. 956420*

The woods and meadows of this parish are threaded by the alluring little Avill river born under Dunkery, lipping its way over pebbles, tumbling noisily over large stones, and flowing with a small tributary stream beneath a single-arched bridge on the Timberscombe—Dunster road. On the way it courses through the paddock of a house called Knowle, now a riding centre. The medieval tenant of an earlier house (by the curious name of Owl Knowle) on this site paid its overlord 'a clove gillyflowre' as rent. It is also on record that Agnes, wife of a Richard Elsworth, a 'husbandman' who rented it, was digging a grave for her stillborn child and unearthed a store of gold nobles, enough to fill a quart pot. She gave two of them to women who had helped her and handed the rest in a 'treen (wooden) dish' to her husband. Valued at £107 they were swiftly claimed as treasure trove by the lord-of-the-manor, and a smaller part by the Crown, so that the lady reaped no profit. Nobles and angels from this store were kept for several centuries at Dunster Castle.

However the Elsworth family prospered. Nearly three centuries

94

later another Elsworth was living at Bickham, the manor house on the road to Wheddon Cross. A medieval house with a chapel stood here before the present dwelling with its handsome facade, its three gables with a roundel in each, its garden enclosed by high red brick walls, its orchards renowned in the 19th century for their cider. This Richard, who died in his early twenties, was a generous benefactor to Timberscombe church. He contributed to the re-building of the tower in 1708, gave a painting for the altar, and endowed a charity school with £10 a year, so the village children might learn to read and write. The school survives in the village street with the original stone plaque over its doorway.

The red sandstone church, dedicated to the Celtic missionary, St. Petrock, houses a number of treasures, that include the medieval door with its wrought iron hinges, handle, and great wood lock; the fan-vaulted screen dividing nave and chancel; a wall painting of King David; two piscinas; and a fine set of handbells. Outside, under the blue-and-gold clockface, a tablet in a sandstone niche bears a much eroded inscription to Richard Elsworth.

From about 1820 until well into the present century, Timberscombe Friendly Society held its colourful procession on the first Tuesday in June. Led by local musicians, members walked to Bickham House, carrying their beautiful floral staves. The master of Bickham entertained them to lunch and cider at tables in front of the house. In later years they walked back to Knowle where ladies 'judged' the staves. Dancing and 'revels' in a field near the church lasted until nightfall.

Clicket is a deserted village lying in ruins in an overgrown valley stretching up towards Luxborough, and reached by a rough track above Timberscombe church. Fifty years ago older people remembered a grandparent or other old person who had been 'christened at Clicket chapel' (a cottage meeting house), had 'played in Clicket band', or disported in the orchard of the farm called Combe. Now bits of broken masonry, portions of old walls, round pillars of cowsheds, fragments of cottages and linhays, and of external bread ovens, can be discovered among fruit trees gone wild, straggling copses, and fallen boughs along the edge of a little stream.

Snowdrop Valley is one of Timberscombe's chief blessings. Public access is allowed subject to 'No picking of Snowdrops' and may this state of affairs long continue! In February this valley is pure delight, lying under scudded cloud, a wind soughing in the bare grey-green woods on the slopes. Down the combe races the exuberant Avill and, almost everywhere are ribbons and sheets of white under lichened larches and grey beeches, among fallen leaves and dark ivy. 'Picturesque, romantic country' wrote Collinson, describing Timberscombe as 'the wooded combe'.

From 1932 until 1966 the Methodist chapel was served by the Rev. John Percival Martin, whose brother, the Rev. keble Martin compiled and illustrated the celebrated *Concise British Flora.* John Percival wrote a number of popular children's books known as the 'Uncle' series after one of their leading characters, an elephant. Undeservedly they have lapsed into obscurity, though some of the titles are now being reprinted.

TIVINGTON   *O.S. 934451*

A steep switchback of a lane, where the hedge banks are patterned by yellow toadflax and pink convolus, leads up to this tiny hamlet composed of cream walls, thatch, brown-tiled roofs and russet-brown farm buildings. For over two centuries dependants of Blackford manor toiled up this lane to hear Mass in the wayside chapel dedicated to St. Leonard, patron of prisoners. After the Reformation a cottage was built on to the east end and the window blocked—the cottage survives and is occupied today. The chapel itself was turned into a barn, but its sturdy sandstone walls survived the onslaughts of man and weather. In the last century Mrs. Jane Kingdom kept a dame school here; and the big fireplace, built of chunks of sandstone, may have been added at that time to provide warmth. The view is a glorious one: tree-dotted pastures and woods, interspersed with red and brown farmsteads, rolling away through distant haze of blue to reach a range of hill slopes that include Dunkery and Robin How dressed in brown, green and purple.

In 1896 the Acland family rescued the building and restored it to Anglican use, giving it a feature unique in the diocese—a roof of Somerset thatch. It is an intimate and endearing place of worship, furnished with many gifts. The red kneelers embroidered in green and blue were worked by the parishioners. The little altar has a rose silk frontal with matching cushion for the Bible. The plain oak seating came from Milverton. The reading desk was made from box pews, once in Selworthy church. Behind the altar there is an Italian tryptych painted with images of the Virgin, Child and Magi; St. Christopher; St. John and the Lamb—this was presented by the late Dr. Francis Eeles, whose expert advice guided later restoration and repairs. A lover of Somerset churches, he is buried at Selworthy, the mother church. Over the door is a bell said to have come from the Acland yacht, *Lady of St. Kilda.*

Blackford manor house, once owned by Edward Wingfield, Royalist and equerry to Charles I's Queen Henrietta Maria, was burned down in 1875. It was sited opposite the Dove Cote, built by a nephew of the Conqueror. Circular with flattened conical roof, hole in the top, without revolving ladder, it is one of the oldest dove cotes in the country.

TREBOROUGH   *O. S. 010364*

This is a high isolated village, wearing an air of desolation when winter winds sweep over the Brendon Hills. Nevertheless several half-ruined cottages have been transformed into attractive homes, while flocks of sheep graze the steep fields, some of the latter snatched from the moorlands—as their gorse thickets and clumps of reeds testify. (Older men can still remember little ricks thatched with reed). There is a feeling of *endurance* about this lonely place, where almost every building is constructed of Brendon stone and—except for recent repairs—roofed with Treborough slate.

In 1820 a party of labourers went into Langridge Wood to dig for stone. Shovelling the loose stones of the cairn, their spades struck a stone slab that proved to be the side of a stone chest *(kist)* covered by a slab lid. Inside they found a man's skelton, crouched with knees drawn up to his chin. They piously re-buried this prehistoric man's bones in Treborough churchyard, although he was born centuries before the founder of Christianity. Part of a prehistoric track runs alongside a hedge and climbs towards the high road on the top. The 'Treborough Man' must have used it. Now it is smothered by teasles, hogweed, hemp agrimony, and layered thick with leaf mould. The high road incorporates most of the Saxon *Herepath* ('army road') that ran east-west over the Brendons.

The church of St. Peter looks as stark as the site. Of ancient origin, mainly Perpendicular in style, with a 19th century pyramid roof on the tower, it has pews for about 100 people. There are a few distinctive features inside which is lightened by clear window glass and cream-washed walls, except for the chancel painted orange. A sculptured wooden figure by Rachel Reckitt, the local artist, is a recent gift. In the churchyard a medieval cross with a modern shaft is surrounded by gravestones bearing local names—such as Chedzoy, Staddon, Southwood—some of whom met their deaths in the slate quarries, while others bear the names of Welshmen employed at the iron mines at Raleghs Cross nearby. The deserted mine workings and buildings were still much in evidence in 1895 when Page described the scene in his *An Exploration of Exmoor*.

The gaunt chimneys, the ugly pumping-houses, do not improve the landscape already rendered sufficiently dreary by the rows of ruinous cottages bordering the roadside. There is in particular a chapel, inscribed 'Beulah' whose blistering walls, boarded windows, and overthrown railings are a sad commentary on its title. A parish doctor told me he could remember the time when over one hundred families of miners occupied the village; now with the exception of half-a-dozen cottages, let at next to nothing, the place is worse than Goldsmith's deserted village.

The scene has mellowed since and Beulah, happily, is in good order. The reader is referred to an article on Treborough in the *Exmoor Review 1967*.

Trentishoe Church

V.B.C.

The slate quarries, beside the hill road running down to Roadwater, were worked on and off for centuries. Maximum production was probably reached in the late 1880s, when more than 30 men were employed. An 1898 price list offered roofing tiles, chimney tops, hearth and shelving stones, steps, staddle stones, window cills, cisterns and head stones. The quarries were finally abandoned in 1938 and have since been used as a Council rubbish dump. In 1981 however, with the encouragement of the landowner, members of the Exmoor Natural History Society took the area in hand and started to clear brambles, cut paths and steps, instal nesting boxes, and fix four benches given by a member. Finally, after much hard and imaginative effort, the site was formally opened in June 1982 as a Conservation Area and dedicated by the Bishop of Bath and Wells.

TRENTISHOE and HEDDON'S MOUTH   O. S. 646486/655497

The wind screamed around Hunters Inn...The sea was less than a mile away. The river flowed below the towering cleave, tameless and unclimbable, its sides grey and smooth with loose flakes of shale. All things in the cleave were hidden as the hounds of the storm bayed across the sky . . . Fed by a hundred torrents, the river rose many feet.

Thus reads the stormy climax of Henry Williamson's splendid story, *The Old Stag,* in which after a six-hour run the stag plunges into the sea at Heddon's Mouth, an event superbly illustrated by Tunnicliffe's woodcut. See the picture on p.120.

Hunters Inn has sheltered countless visitors who go there for a variety of reasons. Artists hope to capture something of the wild territory encompassed by the parishes of Trentishoe and Martinhoe, the rough rolling moors, the swelling downs where prehistoric man raised his barrows, valleys filled with woods, plunging headlands, jagged cliffs dropping sheer to the sea. Anglers come to fish for trout, bird watchers to observe buzzard and kestrel, lapwing and curlew. For the walker there is infinite choice—dizzy cliff paths, tracks twisting over moor and hill, ways through woods beneath boughs of oak, ash and beech beside white, alder-edged streams. S. H. Burton ascribes Heddon to the Celtic word *etin* (giant) and adds:

The valley through which the river flows to the sea seems well fitted to be the abode of legendary monsters . . . The walls are so steep—700 feet high, with a gradient of seven in

99

ten—that, particularly on the western side, little grows, despite the sheltered position that makes the Heddon cleave the warmest valley in North Devon.

Smuggling here was an historical fact. In *Exmoor Review 1962* Margery Oldham tells the story of 'Lucky Jim Muxworthy', while in *Ships and Harbours of Exmoor* Grahame Farr describes 'the Trentishoe haul of 1827', a local *cause célèbre*. Briefly Customs officers and coastguards surrounded Jim Hoyle's farm where, under the stable floors they found 262 tubs of brandy, worth £1,180. In both cases the prisoners escaped through a back window!

Young James Hannington (see under **Martinhoe**) loved all this land, exploring it in every sort of weather, riding over it on his parochial duties. His Exmoor pony never feared cliffs. When appointed curate at Trentishoe, he lived at Hunters Inn, sometimes in discomfort from smoky chimneys. In recent years, J. H. B. Peel, the rural writer, took up occasional residence there, on the invitation of the proprietor to become the 'non-paying tenant of a one-room house on the estate'.

The boy Bradley, author of *Exmoor Memories,* retained rather dismal recollections of his visit to the parsonage at Trentishoe. He found the house very cold with bare boarded floors and the plainest of furniture.

What struck us most was the high frame barricade of timber all round three sides of the little house, and but a few yards from it. This, we learned, was filled with gorse in winter as a protection from the fearful snowstorms which smote this aerial spot.

And he was saddened to observe the life, devoid of rural pleasures like riding and fishing, led by the parson's pale-faced sons and daughters, whose repressive father cooped them up indoors at their books—with Exmoor all around them.

The little church of St. Peter stands high up, but in a hollow. The interior is like a cool cell—white walls, clear window glass, an atmosphere of devotion. By custom a corn dolly hangs next to the Achievement of George V on the panelling of the musician's gallery, which is pierced with a hole for the bass-viol player's bow. William Tucker (1813-1895) played the clarinet and flute, James Brook played another clarinet for 55 years. The small organ came from *S. S. Mauretania,* presented by the Cunard Steam Ship Company in January 1966. A gravestone in the churchyard records that David (Dick) Turpin, who died in 1979 aged 80, was organist for 20 years.

TWITCHEN

From Heasley Mill the road to Twitchen, 'the two-forked way', bends past a little wild place named Badger's Combe, where a lone white cottage hides behind a tangle of beeches near a bridge and the road is wet with small streams. At Twitchen Cross where the stream runs under the road, a peacock struts among the farm buildings of grim grey stone. Ahead swells one of the few unchanged areas of Exmoor, shaggy and brown and steep, close to the cultivated field-slopes that were once as rough and wild. The small plain church of St. Peter and its churchyard face an almost circular prospect coloured green, bronze, blackish brown; and are swept by winds rushing across it. See pictures on pages 116 and 118.

Gravestones repeat the names of several generations of families rooted in the neighbourhood—Buckingham (Lambs Combe Farm), Chapple, Chanter, Moore and Lyddon. Moores and Lyddons inter-married; some of the Lyddons owned Twitchen Mill, and an unusual epitaph from the Book of Job mentions that one, John Lyddon, died in 1896 'Like as a Shock of Corn Cometh in his Season'. This family was probably connected with the staunch Quaker Lyddons of Withiel Florey, who included William Lyddon imprisoned in 1685 (see under **Withiel Florey**). Many Lyddons became faithful Methodists, including the Twitchen branch; the Moores likewise. The Moores, owners of a property called Higher House, may have been converted by John Wesley himself, for we know that he visited North Molton (only about 4 miles away) in 1745 and twice more after that. One of the family inscribed his children's births, starting in 1763, in a copy—still existing—of Wesley's *Notes on the New Testament*. His nephew had twelve children, of whom nine were girls. On dark evenings they worked at embroidery, each with her candle. A sampler survives worked by Tomascine (as her name is spelt on her tombstone). It was she who married John Lyddon, subject of the epitaph above, in about 1850, and who added a chapel on to the house that he and his brother had built. Later Lord Poltimore claimed both of these buildings. The Lyddons were talented and active. John's father William, drove the first stage wagon from Minehead to Bristol and, after returning to Twitchen—as N. V. Allen records in his book about Exmoor places of worship—'laboured ceaselesly for the Methodist cause along the southern edge of Exmoor until his death in 1852'. Another William, who died in 1898, was a versatile craftsman—wheelwright, millstone dresser, organ builder, coffin maker. His jobs took him round many farms and into many houses. From 1844 until 1864 he kept a diary of his rich and varied days, that is a valued possession of his descendants.

Long out of use, Twitchen mill makes a handsome house, still in occupation, black and white and grey like the rest of this tiny village: the disused millstones lying against the wall, little white cascades foaming down the grass banks of the lane.

The old church tower, Upton, before removal of the ivy.

Colin Thornton

UPTON

Sparsely threaded along the eastern end of the road between Wimbleball and Lowtrow Cross, the village clings to the edge of Haddon Hill. Cattle drovers used to tramp this wind-swept ridgeway and call in at Lowtrow Cross Inn, after turning their beasts into a nearby field or leaving them to crop the verges. Another customer was the farrier-cum-vet, a self-taught animal doctor, known also for his skill in pulling human teeth. A regular event here was the annual Rent Audit, at which tenant farmers paid their dues to the lord-of-the-manor or asked for remission in a hard year.

Upton is a little place, with but a few of the amenities that make up a community—church, chapel, garage, shop, and school (now closed), strung along the road. A few houses and farms—built of ragstone from the old Brendon quarries and roofed with Treborough slates—settle into or stand back from the valley of the infant Haddeo. This river rises north-east of Venne House which, in the early 1800s, belonged to Silas Blake, squire of Upton, and collateral descendant of the famous Admiral Blake, whose statue stands in Bridgwater today. Silas Blake's bailiff was one, Martin Marsh, a skilled and trustworthy man and a dedicated Bible Christian, who prevailed on the squire to build a chapel for his growing congregation. After the death of Silas in 1869 and of his widow, two years later, the property passed to the latter's nephew, the Rev. N. H. C. Ruddock, a High Churchman who disliked Dissenters and discovered that the chapel had never been legally conveyed to the Bible Christians. He so engineered things that, for lack of repairs, the building eventually disintegrated, though happily a new stone chapel was put up on a different site in 1878, and stills stands today.

Ruddock's activities did not end there. At his own expense he put up a massive new rectory, far too large for the parish but intended, so it is believed, to serve as a centre for clergy meetings and retreats.It has long since been sold away. Moreover the old parish church of St. James, standing in a farmyard about a mile north-west of the village, was abandoned in 1867 in favour of the present plain building beside the main road. Twelve years later Ruddock, as patron, presented an eccentric character, the Rev. J. Cowden Cole, to the living, on a stipend of only £40 a year, a starvation wage even in those days. In his book, *Memories of a Stag Harbourer,* Fred Goss wrote warmly of Cole as a keen hunting man who, despite his poverty, contrived on hunting days to hire a pony from a local carpenter for five bob a time.

> The pony was not a galloper but it was a stayer, and I can see the old gentleman now, garbed in leggings over his trousers—he never wore breeches—an Inverness cape over his shoulders—never a mackintosh—and a square bowler on his head, plodding away behind the rest. He was always behind, sometimes so far behind that he used to meet the hounds coming back, but I never knew him to give in till news filtered through that the hounds had either killed or abandoned the hunt.

Cole had another interest—an obsession in fact: that of preserving the old church at all costs. He conducted, single handed, a long and hopeless campaign to such effect that in 1899 he was dismissed by a Consistory Court for alleged neglect of duties. Although the nave and chancel were demolished, the tower was allowed to remain and in time was so encased in ivy that it came to look like an immense prehistoric tree. Cole's spirit was doubtless gladdened by the news that, as recently as 1971, a demolition order was resisted and that today, stripped of its ivy, the tower stands in all its stark beauty beside Upton Farm.

An old postscript about Venne House is the story, widely believed in the 1930s, that it was used as a refuge by Col. Charles Lindbergh, his wife and son, after the kidnapping of his 20-month old baby in New Jersey, USA.

WHEDDON CROSS—
See CUTCOMBE

WINSFORD   *O.S. 905350*

The country round Winsford is impregnated with ancient history. For example, in the direction of Exford there are two forts: one at Road Castle, high up on Road Hill, thought to date from Roman times; the other at Staddon Hill, now being invaded by spruce plantations, and originating in the Iron Age. To the west the Wambarrows—grouped burial mounds of Bronze Age chiefs, haunted by the black dog of legend—crown Winsford Hill at just under 1400 feet; while, at Spire Cross, a shelter protects the Caratacus Stone. In her book, *Ancient Exmoor,* Hazel Eardley-Wilmot writes of it:

It bears a Latin inscription, datable to the Dark Ages, which is read as 'carataci nepus'; perhaps 'clansman of Caratacus' would translate it best. So it is commonly called the Caratacus Stone, and assumed to have been erected beside the ridgeway either by or in compliment to Caradoc's relation, somewhere about 500 AD. But while the inscription is certainly of that time, the stone may have stood there much longer. It might have been set for the water-spirit some two thousand years before the Celtic leader's tribesmen passed that way.

People wonder about the Caratacus shelter. It was put up by Sir Charles Acland in 1906, and in 1918 the monument was leased to the National Trust for 500 years. The Stone was scheduled in 1925, thrown down in 1936 by persons unknown, and very carefully re-erected by the Office of Works in 1937.

Winsford Hill, now in the care of the National Trust, acted as a reserve at a critical point in the history of the Exmoor pony breed. Anthony A. Dent wrote in his *The Pure Bred Exmoor Pony:*

The ponies kept on the Royal Forest by the Crown became over the centuries the private property of the Wardens; and as the Wardenship was [normally] hereditary, the ponies were handed down with the rest of the family property. Thus the last Warden, Sir Thomas Acland [10th baronet] felt justified in driving down a selection of the best—before final enclosure—to Winsford Hill, where their descendants may still be seen, branded with the sign of the anchor.

It was a near thing. At this juncture, in 1815, only a dozen pure bred mares, it is believed, were left to continue the line.

And now to Winsford itself which W. H. Hudson described in 1909 as 'fragrant, cool, grey, green—immemorial peace, second to no English village in beauty, running waters, stone thatched cottages, hoary church-tower'. Despite all that has happened since then, the village retains a similar appeal today. 'I never dreamed that such a place could exist', declared a coach passenger from an industrial town. Snowy geese parade on the little green. Hudson's grey and yellow wagtails still trip jauntily on the stones of the ford. People linger on the toylike bridges set over the sparkling Exe or the babbling Winn brook. Thatched roofs still shelter the stone cottages and the Royal Oak Inn, with Charles II's Boscobel oak painted on its sign. A fairly young but sturdy oak, planted on King George V's Silver Jubilee in 1935, flourishes on the daisied green that makes a small public garden.

In his book, *Exmoor: The Riding Playground of England,* Cecil Aldin, the artist, wrote:

I think the Oak at Winsford runs the two Ship inns in the Porlock district very close as regards age . . . a thatched house, having a very thick Somersetshire thatch renewed every few years layer over layer. Rye straw on some of the bottom layers would go to prove its great age. Originally the Oak was just a small village public house and only since the stag-hunting revival has it catered for holiday visitors.

Winsford Church and Village

Iris Hardwick

In the *Exmoor Review 1981,* G. N. C. Swift remembered William Baker's general store that only closed in the 1930s after a long life of service to a closely-knit community of the kind that Jack Hurley, former editor of *The West Somerset Free Press,* knew so intimately and described in the same *Review* number. Swift recalled the blacksmith, Billy Blake—a stout cheerful man with a curious squeaky voice—at his forge near the cobbled packhorse bridge over the Winn—Smithy Bridge preserves the memory.

In the late 19th century farm jobs became scarce and wages stayed abysmally low. A Winsford woman, who went away with her husband and family, returned widowed with eight children and expecting a ninth. This last, born March 1881, was Ernest Bevin, who became a leading trade union leader and a great Foreign Secretary. He was born in the slate-roofed grey cottage opposite the present village shop—a plaque marks it—and his mother supported her family by cleaning at farmhouses and at the Royal Oak. She took her cherished youngest child to the Methodist chapel—now a private house—and sent him on weekdays to the C. of E. primary school. Mr. Dicker, the schoolmaster, took an interest in local history and in 1895 listed the names of Winsford fields: among them, Stately, Larks Lears or Lease, Hymen's Piece, Higher Summerway, Folly, Lady Ford Meadow, Lantern Mead, Peter's Corner, and Lousy Piece, a name referring to pig sties.

The parish church of St. Mary Magdalene is a large building on an eminence above the village, and emphasised by its 80-foot tower. It is notable for several features, including the fact that the nave and aisles are under one external roof, though with separate waggon roofs inside. A succinct account is given in *Churches and Chapels of Exmoor* by N. V. Allen, who also has an interesting note on the Methodist chapel attended by the young Bevin.

WITHIEL FLOREY *O.S. 987334*

This hamlet lies only a mile or two off the main road that runs westward from Raleghs Cross, yet it feels and is remote. The sense of solitude grows as you go along the approach road, shadowed here and there by tall trees and edged in summer with broad bands of willowherb. The little church, Castle Hill Farm next door, and a few other farmsteads make up this scattered settlement, most of it built of rough Brendon Hill stone and Treborough slate, sturdy and unadorned.

Flowering elder surrounds the churchyard in summer. Some of the tombstones are sculptured with old-fashioned motifs like clasped hands. Some are made of local slate. They display quaint pious epitaphs and carry names of families and of farms associated with the dead — Swansea, Barrow, Eastcott, Castle Hill, Withiel. Although devoid of special architectural merit, the church is an endearing building. Its 13th century predecessor, restored in 1871, was within a month of completion partly burnt down. Luckily a labourer saw smoke rising from the tower. Re-building then took place. A few years ago the church had fallen into such a state of decay that visitors were turned back by notices warning them that entry was dangerous. It stood forlorn, and a petition was issued by the Archdeacon of Taunton for its demolition. But the parishioners fought back, began raising money and, with the help of a substantial grant from the Friends of Friendless Churches, found some £3,000 to enable restoration to be carried out. Today its austere whitewashed interior exerts the charm of sheer simplicity, furnished with plain benches, a small pulpit with a stair, a tiny organ, and old brass lamps suspended from the roof. Before 1871 there was a west gallery for the 'Singers', as the little orchestra was called. Summer and winter, across fields or along dark lanes, half-a-dozen musicians carried their instruments to church; bassoon and bass viol, clarinet and hautboy, viol and flute. The congregation turned to face them while singing the hymns. Withiel Florey Singers and choir attained renown and were in demand outside the parish. They were still remembered fifty years ago, as was George Matthews of Leighland who trained them and wrote music for them. Acquisition of a small harmonium ended these pleasant activities—its first players used to carry it home across the fields for practice.

Echoes of Exmoor, Second Series (1924) contains an account of Squire Stawell who ruled the roost at Withiel until his death in about 1838. He was, it seems, a prime example of paternalism, both tyrant and benefactor, working with his men in the fields, admonishing the laggards, befriending the weak and needy. He spoke the King's English and the vernacular with equal ease, and sustained all the old traditions of life and work that dated, many of them, from the distant past. Twenty years or so after his death, the parish was benefiting from the short-lived prosperity, generated by the Brendon Hill iron mines. The terminus of the 'old mineral railway' from Watchet lay inside the parish at Gupworthy where, just off the road, the station house still stands. Remains of the old track, broken bridges, and sealed shafts tell the sad tale of dereliction. Gupworthy Chapel, constructed by Bible Christians from two miners' cottages was used for worship until 1972. A handful of Methodist families took their places on the plain beaches until the very end.

The spirit of Nonconformity has always been strong on the Brendon Hills, and it exhibited itself early and very bravely at Withiel Florey. Throughout the 17th century a few Quakers refused to pay their tithes, assembled for religious meetings in each other's houses, and consequently suffered persecution, fines and sometimes years in prison. Conspicuous among them was the Lyddon family of Swansea Farm, which ultimately was licensed by the Bishop for Quaker worship. Several Lyddons were buried in the Quaker graveyard they had made by dividing off a piece of ground at Swansea Farm; but graves are no longer visible today. The story of the Lyddons' sufferings is told in *Exmoor Review 1980*.

WITHYCOMBE

The Rev. John Collinson, that indefatigable horseman and historian of Somerset, praised Withycombe's situation in 1791: 'a fertile vale encompassed on three sides by lofty, cultivated hills' with a view of the Somerset coast and sea to the North. He found a village of some 43 houses that, apart from the farms, were strung along a single straggling street where a small stream from Rodhuish hill babbled alongside. A noble oak wood crowned a rounded hill. Black game abounded on the hills where wild raspberries and whortleberries grew. Forty years later another traveller mentioned the little stream that turned the mill; the fine oak woods planted by a Luttrell; the commons and sheep walks on Withycombe Hill and Black Hill. He wrote disdainfully of Withycombe's 'two straggling streets of mean houses', deep worn roads, high old-fashioned causeways, while praising its pleasant situation south of the turnpike road at the entrance of a deep valley.

Writing in 1895 Page related how, 'close to the gate opening upon Withycombe common', he found 'the indistinct remains of a large stone circle':

Forty or fifty years ago there were traces of several hut-circles within the walls; but these have now entirely vanished. The tenant at the adjoining farm told me that great quantities of stone had been carted away for draining and like purposes, and that, having cut the fern which grows thickly all over the enclosure, for thirty-six years, he was quite sure there was no sign of a basement remaining.

Today, the situation of Withycombe, well away from the main road and its traffic, gives the village a quality of peace that is rare. It is certainly no place of 'mean' houses. The churchyard on its high knoll commands a vista of brown, pink, red and cream walls, of grey and orange-tiled roofs, and grouped in a pleasing and irregular composition that attracted John William North, the Victorian artist who lived in a house near the church gate, 1904-14. Among numerous pictures he painted here are *Withycombe Church* (now in Bristol Art Gallery), *The Old Yew Tree*, and *Garden and Orchard, Withycombe*.

The little stream slips downward beside the main street and makes a ford where the road turns off to Rodhuish. A lingering visitor can glean grains of local history from inscriptions on the tombstones. One dated 1847, commemorates 'James Leversha of Court Place in this Parish and Izott, wife of the above'. It is likely that James was the descendant of a Leversha, who was one of the Flemish craftsmen employed by the Luttrells to make the beautiful plasterwork ceilings and chimney pieces in Dunster Castle and East Quantoxhead court house. The name Court Place may indicate the site of the manor house.

Betsy Dent, an extremely poor widow of over 80, saintly yet cheerful, lived in a cob-and-thatch cottage, now demolished, near the church and entertained to Sunday tea, in a spotless room adorned with geranium and shining brass, the Methodist preacher who ministered to fervent congregations in a number of Exmoor villages. The chapel is no longer used, and at one time the mill was its neighbour.

The attractive little church, dedicated to St. Nicholas, built in the 13th century, has escaped drastic restoration and is little changed. Its graceful rood screen is one of a group carved by craftsmen who made the lovely Dunster screen. Two striking effigies, almost as old as the church, lie against the north and south walls. One is of a medieval lady wearing a lacy headdress. She lies on the lid of a stone coffin—opened in 1913 and found empty—the heart-case between her hands supposedly denoting burial in another parish. The effigy rests between two most unusual castellated stone candlesticks carved with foliage and masks. The other effigy represents a gentleman of the same period, gowned and wearing—it is said—the earliest hat on such an effigy. Some like to believe that it represents Reginald FitzUrse, one of the murderers of Thomas à Becket in 1169; but as the costume is not that of a mailed knight, the carving must have been done a century after FitzUrse's death.

A brass tablet in the vestry records information upon which a grotesque local legend is based. It concerns Joan Carne, the 17th century mistress of the old house called Sandhill (now Sandhill Farm) that lies under Croydon Hill. The story is told in Jack Hurley's *Legends of Exmoor*. Briefly, it was believed that, since the lady had married and buried three husbands, she had done away with them and was a witch into the bargain. She herself died on 29 October 1612, and was duly interred with full Christian rites. However, the funeral over, mourners started whispering and, on re-entering Sandhill, discovered Joan Carne busily cooking a meal!

Thirty years later is was in this house that the Royalist Colonel Francis Wyndham wrote the letter to Thomas Luttrell who—under pressure from his Roundhead wife was holding Dunster Castle for Parliament—that persuaded Thomas to change allegiance and hand the Castle over to the king. Wyndham in turn held out to the very end of the Civil War.

110

WITHYPOOL

This village lies in the very heart of the Moor and is one of the oldest settlements. There is evidence of prehistoric man in the tumulus and stone circle on Withypool Hill, and at Green Barrow and Brightworthy Barrows on Withypool Common. In historic times it was at Withypool and Hawkridge that the Free Suitors or small farmers held land inside the Royal Forest, to which special rights and duties were attached. These tenants were permitted without charge to keep a stated number of beasts in the Forest, and cut turf, heath and fern : in return for helping the Warden's representative round up cattle, sheep, and horses nine times a year; perambulate or check the boundaries once in seven years; and serve on the coroner's jury if anyone was found dead in the Forest. They also attended the Court or Swainmote held annually at Hawkridge and Landacre (with a brief interval in the 17th century when the Court went to Simonsbath) in order to regulate business. All this came to an end in 1818 when, following enclosure of the Forest, the Free Suitors were allotted an average of 31 acres each. The story is told in full in E. T. MacDermot's *A History of Exmoor Forest* and outlined in *Exmoor Review 1968*.

In the latter publication there is also a short account of Withypool Common where, as elsewhere, the land—though owned by the lord-of-the-manor—was subject to rights of grazing, turf-cutting etc. by neighbouring farms. Business was administered by the Court Leet, usually in comfort at the Royal Oak in Withypool, which survived until 1921, and is now conducted by the Withypool Commoners Association formed in 1949. Following the Commons Registration Act 1965 and the revival of interest in the use of common land, in particular the question of public access, the role of the Association is more important than ever.

As late as the end of the 18th century Withypool was marooned in an ocean of moorland, its roads practically impassable, its inhabitants set apart from all commerce with the outside world. 'An unpleasant and unprofitable parish both to owners and community...little to sell and less to buy', wrote Locke sweepingly (in his *Supplement* to Collinson), adding that labourers fed on 'pottage', while farmers were well-fed on beef and cider. Honey was used instead of sugar; labourers' womenfolk wove wool into blankets and garments for local use. Even as late as 1907 bad roads stopped the transport of iron ore from a mine in Blackland, north-west of the village. Horses were of course the main means of getting about, and numbers of Withypool people today, as well as holiday makers, are riders. Not many years ago the postman carried his letters on horseback, riding rough tracks to the farms.

Sour as the descriptions are as left by Collinson and Locke, both writers paid tribute to the beauty of this parish which has infinite variety. Flowing acres of moorland, clothed with thyme, fern, heather, moor grasses, emerald green bog patches with their special flora; paths winding like narrow ribbons; little glittering streams with many fish and where a kingfisher may be sighted; cleaves, combes, goyals; woods where red deer lie up; a huge heathery common grazed by sheep and the mealy-nosed Exmoor ponies. Not least, the restless willow-hung Barle (hence Withypool's name), the six-arched bridge at the bottom of the village (that replaced another older one about a hundred yards upstream) and the 15th century Landacre Bridge about three miles towards Simonsbath, which figured in *Lorna Doone* in an adventure of Jeremy Stickles. The wild force of a wall of water brought down by the river Barle in the historic flood of 1952 is graphically described by Hazel Eardley-Wilmot in the *Exmoor Review 1981*.

The village is pretty today, with colour-washed cottages and flowery gardens. It has a post office and shop and the Royal Oak inn, where Blackmore sometimes stayed gathering material for his classic tale. The innkeeper's wife, Mrs Tudball, made shirts for him. He sent her strawberry plants from his nursery garden at Teddington. A later writer, Walter Ramond, also sat on the oak settle in the evening, listening to local speech and collecting local lore. In his *Book of Simple Delights* he called it 'The Rose in June' : 'a little farm goes with the house, no mere innkeeper could make a living in this secluded spot'. Raymond, Somerset born, talked to the snail catcher (for a glass factory), hurdle maker, acorn picker, stone crackers, haymakers. His fresh fragrant essays, that ignored the seamier side of village life, were published in periodicals like *The Spectator* and *The Westminster Gazette,* collected in volumes such as *The Book of Crafts and Character.* At Withypool he lived in a homely cottage with a half-door, rented for a shilling a week. In later years the postwoman lived here, and then it fell half-derelict. Now, greatly transformed, its half-door gone but its beams and bread-oven retained, it still belongs to owners who care for it. A plaque

Withypool Bridge

Geoffrey N. Wright

marks it: 'Walter Raymond lived here', and it is called 'Raymond's Cottage'. The cabbage-rose that he loved still grows over the front.

Cecil Sharp came here collecting folk songs and, thanks to Raymond, discovered several including 'The Murder of MacDonald' culled from a gipsy woman, nursing her baby on a heap of stones on the moor. Before the first world war children sang such songs as 'The Trees that do grow high', played singing games, went on nutting picnics in flower-trimmed waggons, danced 'Wave the Handkerchief' and 'Hunt the Squirrel' after Harvest Supper, and garlanded the last sheaf. Women went gleaning and marked their bread dough with a cross.

In 1938 the artist, A. J. Munnings, came to his wife's cottage and roved the moorland, feeling 'free as air'. He rode miles on Pineapple, an old horse once owned by Ernest Bawden, the famous huntsman, stalking herds of ponies. One day when he had forgotten his paint brushes, he painted ponies near Badgery Water with brushes improvised from chewed twigs and teazles.

Among ancient farms held by deep-rooted families is Weatherslade, occupied by generations of Miltons. Fred Milton is a leading breeder of Exmoors. He remembers Walter Raymond, 'with long silver hair', for whom Miltons and their relatives, the Huxtables, were rich sources of information. 'Don't talk to Mr Raymond' said mother to child. 'He'll put you in a book'.

Hope Bourne lives in a caravan and walks several miles to Withypool and back every week, in all weathers, to collect post and shopping. In her books, *Living on Exmoor* and *Wild Harvest,* she has put not only her joy in Exmoor's scenery and seasons, but her satisfaction in grappling with the hardships that life on the Moor can entail. Her weekly column in *The West Somerset Free Press* has delighted many readers.

The little church of St. Andrew, standing back on a rise, and the Methodist chapel (now closed), are described by N. V. Allen in his *Churches and Chapels of Exmoor.*

WOODY BAY—See MARTINHOE

Woody Bay. See p.64

John Keene

WOOTTON COURTENAY   O.S. 938434

In 1943 A. J. Munnings, the artist, was walking as well as painting in his neighbourhood. 'This glorious free country...', he wrote in a letter:

> This week I have been at Wootton Courtenay and walking about between there and Selworthy and Bossington and the sea, and what with the great oaks and woods and holly trees and stern hills . . . well, this is a classic piece of country.

A traveller on one of the roads into the village—the name means 'the place in the woods', while Courtenay refers to the family of the Earls of the Devon who held the manor in the 12th century—can see a wide sweep of red fields, lush pastures, thick woodland, backed by the 'stern hills' described by Munnings. The village straggles along a low spur of Grabbist Hill and looks south to Dunkery and the slopes of Joaney How and Robin How, all crowned with cairns. Paths not far from the church lead to the hamlet of Tivington with its thatched chapel and farms, plantation and common; to Webber's Post, the path winding round the base of Robin How and ultimately bringing into view the woods and waters of the Horner valley; to Dunkery, climbing more arduously over heathery moorland; to Dunster, curving steeply through woods to come in sight of the lovely valley of the Avill—melodious name, an echo of Avalon.

Pretty, with flowers spilling from its gardens over pink stone walls, the village has a thriving air. It boasts an old manor house; an hotel, much patronised by visitors for riding and walking; riding stables; the kennels of the Minehead Harriers; general stores; and the only water-powered pottery in West Somerset.

The church is unusual for several reasons. It stands high above the village street in a churchyard with a black yew and a decapitated cross, both remarked on by Collinson, the historian of Somerset, in 1791. Like Luxborough church it has a saddleback tower, altered to that shape in 1866 when the chancel was rebuilt and the south porch added. Although it saved the main structure probably, the restoration was responsible for some sad losses—an early pulpit, west gallery, and old pews, among other things. But the interior is white and light, often fragrant with roses and lilies from local gardens. Two of the pillars have canopied niches—an uncommon feature—regrettably denuded of their original images of St. Lawrence and St. Christopher. The West Country waggon roofs add glory to the building, embellished with carved oak bosses depicting St. George and the Dragon, the Pelican in Piety, an angel, the eagles of St. John. The chancel and tower screens were carved by local hands in 1921.

Reading about life here a century ago is like entering another world, and it had its harsher side. Poor men with donkeys hauled iron from a new mine to Minehead for shipment to South Wales. Others earned a mere 9 shillings a week for felling trees for the Mineral Railway that ran between Watchet and Brendon Hill; and were grateful to exchange this toil for a job in the mines at 2s 6d a day. In summer children might earn a few shillings picking whortleberries—a welcome supplement to the family wage. Tom Court, a gardener who lived most of his life in the village, wrote an entertaining account of 'urt picking' in the *Exmoor Review 1967.*

It was everyone's ambition to get a full basket. This didn't often happen, only on a few occasions when whorts were plentiful, or, as we termed it, "they were black hail", did we succeed.

The first place where whorts ripened was on Grabbist. Not a favourite place as the berries grew between gorse and fingers and legs were sore at the end of the day, so we were always glad when the whorts were ripe on Dunkery.

The whorts were sold to Mr Tom Webber and his sister, who had a horse and open cart, in which small barrels were carried.

Whorts were measured into quart pots at the price of 4d a quart at the beginning of the season, dropping to 3d or 2½d as they became more plentiful. During the war the price rose to 2s 6d.

Money earned was used to buy clothes for the winter...We were allowed to keep what money we earned on the last day of whorting, so we were usually very energetic that day!

Skyline at Cussacombe. See p.101

Joan Gifford

Select Book List

Anne Acland	*A Devon Family*	Phillimore
N. V. Allen	*Churches and Chapels of Exmoor*	Exmoor Press
	The Waters of Exmoor	Exmoor Press
	The Birds of Exmoor	Exmoor Press
R. D. Blackmore	*Lorna Doone*	Collins
Hope Bourne	*Living on Exmoor*	Dent
A. G. Bradley	*Exmoor Memories*	Methuen
S. H. Burton	*Exmoor*	Hale
Charles E. H.		
Chadwyck Healey	*A History of Part of West Somerset*	Sotheran
Rev. J. F. Chanter	*A History of the Parishes of Lynton and Countisbury*	Commin
Rev. John Collinson	*History and Antiquities of the County of Somerset:* with *Supplement* by R. Locke	Crutwell Barnicott
Charles Palk Collyns	*Notes on the Chase of the Wild Red Deer*	Longman
Cicely E. Cooper	*Memoirs of Selworthy and West Somerset*	Cox
Glyn Court	*West Somerset in times Past*	Countryside Publication
Rev. Lewis H. Court	*The Romance of a Country Circuit*	Hooks
Hazel Eardley-Wilmot	*Ancient Exmoor*	Exmoor Press
Grahame Farr	*Ships and Harbours of Exmoor*	Exmoor Press
Fred Goss	*Memories of a Stag Harbourer*	Witherby
C.G. Harper	*The Somerset Coast*	Chapman & Hall
E. W. Hendy	*Wild Exmoor Through the Year*	Cape
W. H. Hudson	*Afoot in England*	Dent
Jack Hurley	*Legends of Exmoor*	Exmoor Press
	Murder and Mystery on Exmoor	Exmoor Press
	Rattle His Bones	Exmoor Press
	Snow and Storm on Exmoor	Exmoor Press
Richard Jefferies	*Red Deer*	Longman
	Jefferies' England	Constable
Rev. W. W. Joyce	*Echoes of Exmoor*	
	Nos. 1 - 3	Simpkin Marshall
	No. 4	Barnes
Berta Lawrence	*A Somerset Journal*	Westaway
	Coleridge and Wordsworth in Somerset	David & Charles
E. T. MacDermot	*The History of the Forest of Exmoor*	Wessex Press/ David & Charles
Rev. H. J. Marshall	*Exmoor Sporting and Otherwise*	Eyre & Spottiswoode
Laurence Meynell	*Exmoor*	Hale
Roger Miles	*The Trees and Woods of Exmoor*	Exmoor Press
C. S. Orwin and		
R. J. Sellick	*The Reclamation of Exmoor Forest*	David & Charles
J. Ll. W. Page	*An Exploration of Exmoor*	Seeley
J. H. B. Peel	*Portrait of Exmoor*	Hale
A. G. Pointon	*Methodists in West Somerset*	Privately published

Twitchen Church and Village. See p.101.

Joan Gifford

Combe Sydenham House. See p.66.

H H Hole